Handbook of Transfusion Medicine

Blood Transfusion Services
of the United Kingdom

THIRD EDITION 2001

Editor: D B L McClelland

London: The Stationery Office

Published by TSO (The Stationery Office) and available from:

Online
www.tso.co.uk/bookshop

Mail, Telephone, Fax & E-mail
TSO
PO Box 29, Norwich, NR3 1GN
Telephone orders/General enquiries: 0870 600 5522
Fax orders: 0870 600 5533
E-mail: book.orders@tso.co.uk
Textphone 0870 240 3701

TSO Shops
123 Kingsway, London, WC2B 6PQ
020 7242 6393 Fax 020 7242 6394
68-69 Bull Street, Birmingham B4 6AD
0121 236 9696 Fax 0121 236 9699
9-21 Princess Street, Manchester M60 8AS
0161 834 7201 Fax 0161 833 0634
16 Arthur Street, Belfast BT1 4GD
028 9023 8451 Fax 028 9023 5401
18-19 High Street, Cardiff CF10 1PT
029 2039 5548 Fax 029 2038 4347
71 Lothian Road, Edinburgh EH3 9AZ
0870 606 5566 Fax 0870 606 5588

TSO Accredited Agents
(see Yellow Pages)

and through good booksellers

Web access

This publication is also available on The Stationery Office website at: https://www.the-stationery-office.co.uk/nbs/handbook2001/index.htm

First published 2001
Second impression 2002

ISBN 011 322427 3

Printed in the United Kingdom for The Stationery Office

Simple Standards for Safe Transfusion

Hospitals should be able to show that they comply with these or similar short, simple statements of some of the essentials of safe transfusion

- There should be a transfusion guideline. This should include indications for transfusion and the laboratory observations to be checked and acted on before and following transfusion.

- The reason for transfusing each patient should be written in the patient's case notes.

- For planned surgery the arrangements for pre-operative assessment should permit correction of medically treatable deficiencies (anaemia, coagulopathy) whenever possible.

- Wrist-bands MUST be worn by all patients who are to undergo transfusion until the transfusion is completed. For out-patients these should be applied on arrival at the clinic/day-ward.

- Anyone who prescribes, orders or administers blood must have had documented training in safe transfusion practice. This training should be refreshed at intervals of not greater than two years.

- Patients should be monitored during the transfusion according to a simple and do-able procedure.

Contents

Pre-transfusion procedures – to ensure donation and patient are compatible
  Type and screen (also called 'group and hold' or 'group and save')
  Red cell compatibility testing (crossmatching)
  'Computer crossmatch'
Blood ordering for planned procedures
  Surgical blood ordering schedule for red cells
  Further red cell transfusion
  Compatibility problems
Storage and collection of red cells for transfusion
Administering blood components and blood products
  Identity checks
  Inspection
  Record keeping and observations
  Adverse reactions
Time limits for infusing blood components
  Red cells
  Platelets
  Plasma
Blood administration sets and equipment
  Red cells, plasma and cryoprecipitate
  Platelets
  Infants and small children
  Cannulas
  Filtration
  Infusion pumps
  Blood warmers
Do not add other pharmaceuticals to blood products

Thrombocytopenia
Neonatal alloimmune thrombocytopenia (NAIT)

11 Haemolytic disease of the newborn

Screening for HDN in pregnancy
Prevention of HDN: the use of RhD immunoglobulin (anti-D)
Indications for anti-D immunoglobulin, in a mother who is Rh D negative
    Administration of anti-D
Routine antenatal prophylaxis with anti-D
Management of HDN: refer early to a specialist unit

12 Adverse effects of transfusion

Surveillance and reporting
    Immediate reporting
    Serious Hazards of Transfusion (SHOT) reporting system
Acute transfusion reactions
    Acute haemolytic transfusion reaction
    Infusion of the contents of a blood pack contaminated by bacteria
    Transfusion-related acute lung injury (TRALI)
    Fluid overload
    Severe allergic reaction or anaphylaxis
Signs and symptoms of severe accute reactions
Management of acute transfusion reactions
Management of severe acute reaction
    Hypotension
    Sustained hypotension
    Antibiotics
    DIC
    If anaphylaxis or a severe allergic reaction is suspected
    If TRALI is suspected
    If fluid overload is suspected
Reactions due to red cell antibodies other than anti-A and anti-B
    Delayed haemolytic reaction
Febrile non haemolytic transfusion reactions
Allergic reactions
Delayed complications of transfusion
    Graft-versus-host-disease (GvHD)
    Iron overload
    Uncharacterised effects on outcome: possible role of immune modulation by transfusion
Post-transfusion purpura (PTP)
    Management

Disclaimer

Whilst the information and advice contained in this handbook is believed to reflect current best clinical practice, neither authors nor publisher can accept any legal responsibility for any errors or omissions.

WHO terminology is used in this handbook

Blood product	Therapeutic substance prepared from human blood
Blood component	Platelets Red cells Fresh frozen plasma Cryoprecipitate White cells
Plasma derivative	Plasma proteins prepared from pooled human plasma under pharmaceutical manufacturing conditions [coagulation factors, immunoglobulin albumin etc]

1
Introductory information

Purpose of this handbook

This book is to help the many people involved in blood transfusion to make sure that when transfusion is needed, the right product is given to the right patient at the right time. The following all play an essential part:

- Medical staff, who assess the patient and *prescribe* and order the product.
- Laboratory or pharmacy staff, who r*eceive the order and prepare the product*, ensuring that it is compatible with the patient.
- Porters and transport personnel, who *collect and deliver* samples to the blood bank and the blood to the patient.
- *Nurses and other clinicians*, who carry out the checks before blood is administered and observe the patient during and after the transfusion.
- Telephone operators, who may have to *make vital contacts in an emergency*.
- Managers, who *provide the facilities and resources* to enable safe transfusion practice.

Evidence-based practice?

Correctly used, blood and blood products can save lives and provide clinical benefit to many patients. However, many aspects of blood transfusion practice have not been rigorously proved by clinical trials so it is impossible to give a completely evidence-based account. We have tried to use the best available evidence about effective treatment. Where good evidence is not available, we have tried to give a balanced view of current opinion about good clinical practice.

In the UK in 2001, thinking about transfusion is strongly influenced by concern about the risk that variant Creutzfeldt-

Jakob disease could be transmitted by transfusion. This is one of many reasons to prescribe blood only when evidence or experience give confidence that it will improve the patient's outcome.

In other parts of the world, clinical decisions about transfusion must take account of differences in the local situation, for example, the epidemiology of transfusion-transmissible infectious diseases and the availability of safe donors and tested donations.

Key topics

Many common problems with transfusion that cause delays and may put the patient at risk are caused by poor communication or failure to use procedures that should be simple, well documented and for which staff need to be trained. Responsibility for ensuring that the procedures and staff training are kept up to date and available rests with the hospital's management.

Vigilance

Some rarer complications of transfusion, such as the transmission of viral infections, may only be recognisable weeks or months after the blood product has been given. Clinical staff have the responsibility of recognising, managing and reporting problems of this type to the hospital blood bank. It is the task of the producer (the Blood Service or other manufacturer of the blood product) to ensure that the products supplied are as safe and as efficacious as possible. The blood bank or Hospital Transfusion Committee staff should ensure that reported adverse events are effectively followed up.

Recent history

Since the 1970s, the viruses that cause hepatitis B, AIDS (HIV) and hepatitis C have been identified. In each case effective tests were quickly developed and introduced to detect and exclude blood donations that could transmit these infections to a recipient. As a result, the risk of being infected with any of these viruses as a result of a transfusion in the UK is now very low. However, we must not forget that some patients, who received transfusions before these tests were available, have suffered very serious consequences of these infections. This is a constant reminder of the need to be alert to the risk of any other infection - perhaps previously unrecognised or unknown - that could be transmitted by transfusion.

Variant Creutzfeldt-Jakob disease

Variant Creutzfeldt-Jakob disease (vCJD) was first described in 1996 in the UK. It differs from the long-recognised sporadic and familial forms of CJD (relatively young age at presentation, differences in clinical features including behavioural change, dysaesthesia and ataxia and relatively slow clinical progression). There is good scientific evidence that vCJD in humans is closely related to bovine spongiform encephalopathy (BSE). The infection is presumed to be acquired through the diet. The current incidence of new cases of vCJD is 12-15 patients per annum. The number of individuals incubating the disease is not known.

A number of features of vCJD suggest the possibility of transmission by blood. It is not known whether vCJD will prove to be transmissible between humans by blood products but the risk cannot be excluded. Therefore, precautions have been taken in the UK. These include the removal of white cells from all clinical blood components and obtaining plasma for fractionation from countries other than the UK. Several other countries have decided that people who have spent periods of time in the UK before 1996 should not donate blood. There is, in April 2001, neither a validated blood-screening test nor effective therapy for this disease. Further precautionary measures may well be introduced in the UK. *The most important way of avoiding risks of transfusion is to prescribe blood products only when they are really needed.*

There is no evidence that *sporadic or familial CJD* has been transmitted by blood transfusion.

2
Production of blood products: from donor to patient

The concept of blood component therapy

It is useful for the prescriber to understand a few basic facts about how blood is collected and processed because this affects the safety and availability of the products. Figure 1 illustrates the processing of blood from donor to patient. Blood is a raw material from which a range of therapeutic products including platelet concentrates, red cell concentrates and fresh plasma is made. Large amounts of plasma are also needed for the production of plasma derivatives, such as albumin, coagulation factors and immunoglobulins.

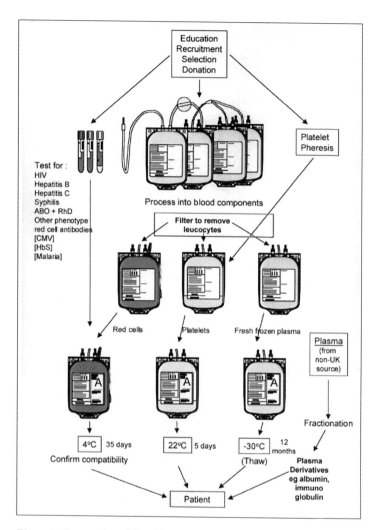

Test for :
HIV
Hepatitis B
Hepatitis C
Syphilis
ABO + RhD
Other phenotype
red cell antibodies
[CMV]
[HbS]
[Malaria]

Education
Recruitment
Selection
Donation

Platelet
Pheresis

Process into blood components

Filter to remove
leucocytes

Red cells   Platelets   Fresh frozen plasma

Plasma
(from
non-UK
source)

Fractionation

4°C   35 days   22°C   5 days   -30°C   12 months   Plasma
Derivatives
eg albumin,
immuno
globulin

Confirm compatibility   (Thaw)

Patient

Figure 1 : Preparation of Blood Components

Blood donors: selection, donation and testing

- Donors can give 450 ml of whole blood, generally up to three times per year.
- Platelets, plasma and red cells can be prepared from whole blood donations or collected by apheresis.

The medical selection of donors is intended to exclude anyone whose blood might harm the recipient, for example by transmitting infection, or who might possibly be harmed by donating blood. In the UK every blood donation is tested for evidence of hepatitis B, hepatitis C, HIV-1, HIV-2 and syphilis. In other countries, different tests for infection may also be needed, depending on the frequency of infection in the community. Each donation is tested to determine the ABO and Rh D blood group. Because of concerns about vCJD, some countries currently exclude from donation individuals who have resided in the UK over the period of the BSE epidemic. At least one country also excludes from donation anyone who has previously received a blood component transfusion.

- Healthy persons aged 17-70 can donate
- First time donations may be taken up to 60 yrs of age
- Donation may be

Whole blood:	2-3 times per year
Plateletpheresis:	Up to 24 times per year
- Autologous donation: Page 43
- Donation by relatives or friend: (directed donation) See page 121

Preparation of blood components from whole blood donations

Blood is collected into sterile plastic packs that are centrifuged to separate red cells, platelets and plasma (Figure 1). In the UK, all the components made from each donation are filtered to remove white cells.

Manufacture of plasma derivatives

These are partially purified therapeutic preparations of human plasma proteins. They are manufactured, in a large-scale pharmaceutical process, from large volumes of plasma. Typically the plasma from at least 20,000 individual donations (about 5000 kg of plasma) is processed by the addition of ethanol and exposure to varying temperature, pH and ionic strength to precipitate different groups of proteins. Further purification and virus inactivation steps are carried out. The final products are solutions or freeze-dried powders.

Since plasma from any one of the individual donors who contribute to each batch of products could introduce infectious agents, careful testing of every donation is vital. Even with testing, some viruses could find their way into the pooled plasma, so the processes include steps to inactivate those that might escape detection. Currently, the plasma of UK donors is not fractionated. Plasma is imported into the UK for fractionation.

Blood product labels

All blood products carry labels applied by the manufacturers. They give information that is important for staff who administer products and also allow the origins of the product to be traced.

Blood components supplied for transfusion should have a blood component label applied by the Blood Service and a 'compatibility label' that is applied by the hospital blood bank (Figure 2). The latter carries information that uniquely identifies the patient for whom the component has been selected. An essential check before infusing any blood component is to make sure that the details on the compatibility label match exactly with the identity of the patient.

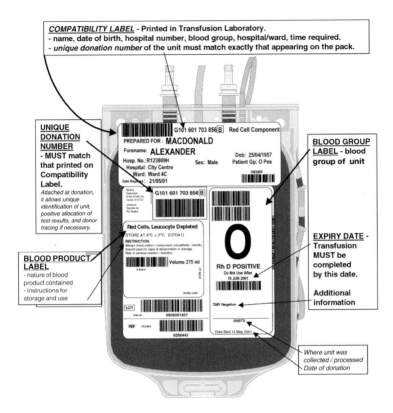

COMPATIBILITY LABEL - Printed in Transfusion Laboratory.
- name, date of birth, hospital number, blood group, hospital/ward, time required.
- *unique donation number* of the unit must match exactly that appearing on the pack.

UNIQUE DONATION NUMBER
- **MUST match that printed on Compatibility Label.**
Attached at donation, it allows unique identification of unit, positive allocation of test results, and donor tracing if necessary.

BLOOD PRODUCT LABEL
- nature of blood product contained
- instructions for storage and use

G101 601 703 856 B   Red Cell Component
PREPARED FOR : MACDONALD
Forename: ALEXANDER
Hosp. No.:R123809H   Dob: 25/04/1957
Hospital: City Centre   Sex: Male   Patient Gp: O Pos
Ward: Ward 4C
Date Required : 21/05/01

G101 601 703 856 B

Red Cells, Leucocyte Depleted
STORE AT 4°C ± 2°C (CPDA1)
INSTRUCTION
Always check patient / component compatibility / identity
Inspect pack for signs of deterioration or damage
Risk of adverse reaction / infection.

Volume 275 ml

LOT   0900001437

REF   733-940
      0200441

BLOOD GROUP LABEL - blood group of unit

O

Rh D POSITIVE
Do Not Use After
19 JUN 2001

CMV Negative

SNBTS
Date Bled 15 May 2001

EXPIRY DATE - Transfusion MUST be completed by this date.

Additional information

*Where unit was collected / processed
Date of donation*

Figure 2 : Blood pack with blood component label and compatibility label

3

Core information about blood components, plasma derivatives and new products

General information

All donations are tested serologically to detect HIV-1 and HIV-2, hepatitis B, hepatitis C and syphilis.

Blood components tested and negative for cytomegalovirus (CMV) antibody are available for immunosuppressed patients and neonates.

Virus inactivated fresh frozen plasma (FFP) is now available (see Table 4).

Red cells and platelets are not subjected to a specific virus inactivation step.

Bacterial contamination of platelets or red cells is extremely rare but can be lethal for the recipient of a contaminated pack. Consider the possibility of this in cases of high fever or unexplained hypotension during or after transfusion.

All blood components have white cells removed as a precaution against variant Creutzfeldt-Jakob disease. The residual leucocyte count is $<5 \times 10^6$ in >99% components (95% statistical confidence). The implications of this are:

- platelet recipients need not be routinely pre-medicated against febrile reactions unless reactions are recurrent and troublesome
- the risk of CMV transmission is reduced
- no further filtration is needed before transfusion (although a standard blood administration set with a screen filter should always be used).

Tables 1-6 provide a summary of information about blood components and plasma derivatives available in the UK. Quality assurance procedures are designed to maintain compliance with these specifications.

Table 1: Blood components - storage and administration

	Red cells Red cells (additive) Whole blood	Platelet concentrate recovered or apheresis	Fresh frozen plasma	Cryoprecipitate
Storage temperature	2 to 6°C	At 20-24°C on a special agitator rack	-30°C	-30°C
Shelf life	35 days	5 days	1 year (frozen)	1 year (frozen)
Longest time from leaving controlled storage to completing infusion	5 hours	Depends on preparation method: consult supplier	4 hours	4 hours
Compatibility testing requirement	Must be compatible with recipient ABO and Rh D type	Preferably ABO identical with patient. Rhesus negative females under the age of 45 years should be given Rh D negative platelets	FFP and cryoprecipitate should be ABO compatible to avoid risk of haemolysis caused by donor anti-A or anti-B	
Points to Note: Administration	• **Infuse through a blood administration set - use a fresh set when administering each infusion of platelets**			
	• **Record details of each blood component infusion in the patient's case record.**			
	• **Follow local procedures or protocols for ordering and administering blood components.**			

Table 2: Red cells

Unit	Red cells in additive solution leucocyte depleted	Red cells, leucocyte depleted	Whole blood, leucocyte depleted
		1 donation	
Volume * ml	550±70	270±50	470±50 including 63 ml antocoagulant
Haematocrit %	0.50 - 0.70	0.55-0.75	0.35-0.45
Haemoglobin g/pack	>40g	>40g	>40g
White cells per unit	< 5 x 10^6 *	< 5 x 10^6 *	< 5 x 10^6 *
Content per unit * Sodium mmol Fresh* Expiry	20 15	15 10	50 55
*Potassium mmol Fresh Expiry	0.5 5	0.3 6	1 9
*Lactate mmol Fresh Expiry		1 10	

Table 2:	Red cells continued		
*Hydroxyl Fresh Expiry	2 10	5 12	20 55
Added chemicals**	Adenine Mannitol Glucose Sodium Chloride (SAGM)	Citrate Phosphate Dextrose Adenine (CPDA)	Citrate Phosphate Dextrose Adenine (CPDA)
Points to Note:	Not recommended for exchange or large volume transfusion of neonates	Usually available only for infants	The large volume of plasma increases risk of hypervolaemia and cardiac failure in susceptible patients.

Dose of 4ml/kg raises venous Hb by about 1g/dl. Typical values are given. For full product specifications, consult supplier user guide

** Additive solutions are used to resuspend packed red cells after plasma is removed They are designed to maintain the red cells in good condition during storage. There are various formulas. A widely used additive solution contains saline, adenine, glucose and mannitol (SAGM).

Sources: Council of Europe Guide to the preparation, use and quality assurance of blood components
7th edition, 2001
Guidelines for the blood transfusion services in the UK, 4th edition, 2001
Quality monitoring data SNBTS

Table 3: Platelets

	platelets, buffy coat derived, leucocyte depleted (random donor)	Platelets, apheresis, leucocyte depleted (single donor)	HLA/HPA compatible apheresis platelets	Crossmatched apheresis platelets
Unit	A pool derived from 4 buffy coats.		1 Donation	
*Volume	up to 300 ml of plasma	Check local product specification.		
Content of platelets	>240 x 10⁹ per donation		>240 x 10⁹	
Content of white cells	< 5 x 10⁶	< 5 x 10⁶	< 0.8 x 10⁹	
Points to Note: Prescribing	. .		Donors are selected to match recipient for some HLA or HPA antigens. May be effective in patients who do not respond to platelets due to HLA or HPA antibodies.	Donors are selected by a test for reaction with recipient's plasma. May be effective in patients who do not respond to platelets due to HLA antibodies.
		Contain sufficient volume (2-300ml) of a single donor's plasma, to cause haemolysis if the donors has potent red cell antibodies. Donor should be ABO compatible.		
	Adult dose 1 pool.		Adult dose: 1 donation	

Typical volumes are given.

Table 4: Fresh frozen plasma cryoprecipitate and cryosupernatant

	Recovered (random donor) FFP, leucocyte depleted	Apheresis (single donor), FFP, leucocyte depleted	Cryosupernatant plasma, leucocyte depleted	Cryoprecipitate, leucocyte depleted
Volume ml	150-300 plasma containing CPDA	300-600 ml of plasma containing CPDA	150-250 ml	10-20 ml
WBC		< 5 x 10⁶/unit		
*Electrolytes: Sodium mmol Potassium mmol Citrate mmol Lactate mmol Hydroxyl mmol	Content per unit: 35 1 4 1 12	Content per unit: 35 1 4 1 12	Content per unit: 35 1 4 1 12	Content per pool of 10 units 20 1 2 1 12
Fibrinogen Factor VIII Other clotting factors	2-5 mg/ml >0.7 IU/ml in >75% packs >0.7 IU/ml	2-5 mg/ml >0.7 IU/ml in >75% packs >0.7 IU/ml	Low content of fibrinogen, factor VIII and vWF factor Used for plasma exchange in TTP	Fibrinogen 150-300mg/pack Factor VIII 80-120 u/pack von Willebrand Factor 80-120 IU/pack
Other plasma proteins		As in slightly diluted plasma.		
Added chemicals		citrate phosphate dextrose adenine		
Points to Note: Prescribing	• Risk of volume overload due to protein content. • Occasional severe anaphylactic reactions, especially with rapid infusion rates. • Infection risks are similar to those of other blood components but plasma components do not transmit CMV or HTLV. • Contain normal levels of plasma immunoglobulins: including red cell antibodies that can damage recipient's red cells.			Use virus inactivated clotting factor concentrates in preference whenever it is possible.

*Typical values are given

Table 5: Fresh frozen plasma variants compared: standard, methylene blue treated, solvent/detergent treated			
	Standard FFP	Methylene blue FFP	Solvent detergent FFP
Source	UK donors, all previously virus tested.* Single unit format.	UK donors, all previously virus tested.* Single unit format.	Non-UK donors; pools of up to 380 litres (600-1,500 ABO identical donations)
Donation testing: serology: genomic	HIV, HBV, HCV HCV	HIV, HBV, HCV HCV	HIV, HBV, HCV, HAV, HCV
Virus risk HIV 1 + 2 Hepatitis C	see page 104	No proven cases reported	No reported transmissions
Hepatitis B			
Hepatitis A Parvovirus B19	Rare event. Rare event.	No greater than for standard FFP. None reported to date.	None reported. Batch withdrawals due to possible B19 content. Seroconversion in patients no greater than with untreated FFP.
Volume	180-300 mls + 50 ml paediatric size.	235-305 mls + 50 ml paediatric size.	200mls; no paediatric size.
Coagulation factor content	Variable between units.	Variable between units.	Constant within batch.
* A decision may be made to import FFP.			

Table 5(cont.): Fresh frozen plasma variants compared: standard, methylene blue treated, solvent/detergent treated

	75% units >0.7 iu/ml fVIII	75% units fVIII >0.5 iu/ml; all other factors >0.5iu/ml; no reduction ATIII, protein C, protein S. No coagulation factor/complement activation.	All factors >0.5 iu/ml.
Cryoprecipitate/cryosupernatant	Available	May become available	Not available
Residual additives	None	<0.05µg/ml MB after MB removal step. No toxicity seen or predicted at this level, even in premature neonates.	<2µg/ml TNBP*; <5µg/ml Triton-X 100. Residual levels not toxic.
Allergic reactions	May be reduced by leucocyte depletion	Reactions attributable to cells would be expected to be reduced.	Probably less frequent
mild	1%		
severe	0.1%		
Adverse reactions due to antibody			Pooling reduces all of these risks
red cell	avoidable	As for standard FFP	
TRALI	5 cases in 2 years (SHOT)		
thrombocytopenia	very rare		
Cellular content	Leucocyte depleted; Rh D matching recommended.	Leucocyte depleted; Rh D matching recommended.	No intact cells or fragments; no need to Rh D match
Product Licence	Not required	Medical device; CE marked	Licensed, batched product
Indications	See BCSH Guidelines	As for FFP	As for FFP
Usage to date	300,000 units/year in UK	>1,000,000 units in Europe	3,000,000 units in Europe

*TNBP: tri (N-butyl) phosphate

Table 6: Human plasma derivatives (as a precaution against vCJD, these are not currently manufactured from UK plasma)

	Human albumin	Human immunoglobulin		Clotting factor concentrates			
		For intramuscular use	For intravenous use	Factor VIII	Factor IX	Prothrombin complex concentrate	Others include
Unit	Usually 20g as 400 ml of 5% solution or 100 ml of 20% solution	Varies with product and supplier.		Typically 250-500 iu in each vial			
Active constituents include:	Human albumin	Human IgG -from a large pool of unselected donors - or from donors with high levels of anti RhD or anti-viral antibodies		Factor VIII	Factor IX	Factors II, IX, X. Factor VII contain some products.	FEIBA (Factor VIII bypassing activity concentrate Factor VII Antithrombin III Fibrinogen Fibrin sealant (Recombinant Factor VIII) (Recombinant Factor VIIa)
Other constituents include:	Sodium: 130-150 mmol/l Other plasma proteins. Stabiliser	Other immuno-globulins and other plasma proteins	Other immuno-globulins and other plasma proteins. Sucrose, pepsin.	Other human plasma proteins			See suppliers' information.

Table 6 (cont.) Human plasma derivatives

	(sodium caprylate)					
Main clinical uses	Hypoproteinaemic oedema with nephrotic syndrome (20%) Ascites in chronic liver disease (20%) Acute volume replacement (5%)	Prophylaxis of specific virus infections such as hepatitis A, B, varicella zoster. Prevention of anti-Rh D antibodies in at risk mothers.	Treatment of inherited and acquired deficiencies of antibody formation. Treatment of immunological disorders such as auto-immune thrombocytopenia purpura (AITP)	Treatment of haemophilia A.	Treatment of haemophilia B.	Replacement of multiple clotting factor deficiencies.	See supplier's information.
Points to Note: Prescribing	20% solution: hyperoncotic and expands plasma volume by more than the amount infused. 5% solution: use carefully - if patient is at risk of sodium retention.	See page 76,89	CAUTION: Risk of Renal failure see page 71		See page 59 All these products should be used under the guidance of a specialist clinician.		
Storage	Store at room temperature.	Storage usually at 4°C but check manufacturers' information					

New Products

Alternative oxygen-delivering fluids ('artificial blood')

Perfluorocarbon and haemoglobin solutions are likely to become available for special clinical indications and may have potential for reducing the need for red cell transfusion for some patients.

Perfluorocarbon oxygen carriers

The active molecule is an inert carbon chain with fluoride and bromide atoms attached. Perfluorocarbon solutions do not have the sigmoid oxygen dissociation curve of haemoglobin, and can only carry useful concentrations of oxygen at very high inspired oxygen concentrations. This limits their use to situations when respiratory support is available. Human volunteers have reported mild 'flu type reactions when receiving perfluorocarbon solutions, possibly due to release of cytokines.

Perfluorocarbons are potentially useful for providing a short-lived improvement in oxygen delivery to tissues and have been evaluated as an adjunct to acute haemodilution (page 45). Another potential application is in emergency resuscitation until compatible blood is available. Despite the short duration of oxygen carrying activity, the perfluorocarbon is excreted only slowly, by exhalation, and it accumulates in RE tissues. Long-term toxicity is unknown.

Haemoglobin (Hb) solutions

There are several products approaching clinical availability. They have good oxygen carriage and offloading, low viscosity, long storage life and no red cell antigens, so no compatibility testing is needed. Because free Hb is nephrotoxic, clinical products are processed to form polymers. Clinical studies have demonstrated adequate oxygen delivery by infused Hb solutions when the patient has an extremely low haematocrit.

A persistent problem during development of these products has been vasoconstriction and hypertension, probably due to binding of nitric oxide. Products now in trial appear to have overcome this. Hb polymers are rapidly metabolised so their therapeutic effect is short. Breakdown of the infused Hb raises bilirubin levels. The red colour of the solutions interferes with many routine clinical chemistry tests and can cause difficulties in management.

Oxygen-carrying solutions will probably soon be licensed for some specific clinical indications. As long as the limitations of these solutions are understood and the potential for side effects recognised, they are likely to provide a means whereby some patients can avoid the need for red cell transfusion. New clinical guidelines for their use will be required

Recombinant Factor VIIa in acquired coagulation disorders

Recent reports suggest that recombinant Factor VIIa may have a role in the management of acute haemostatic failure and may therefore be a potential alternative to fresh frozen plasma in some situations.

Fibrinogen concentrate (virus inactivated)

This product is available, but not licensed in the UK. Subject to the results of clinical trials this may provide an alternative to FFP or cryoprecipitate in some situations.

4

Basics of red cell compatibility

The ABO and Rh D blood groups and antibodies

ABO blood groups

There are four different ABO groups, determined by whether or not an individual's red cells carry the A antigen, the B antigen, both A and B or neither.

> *Normal healthy individuals, from early in childhood, make antibodies against A or B antigens that are not expressed on their own cells.*
>
> people who are group A   have anti-B antibody in their plasma
> people who are group B   have anti-A antibody
> people who are group O   have anti-A and anti-B antibody
> people who are group AB   have neither of these antibodies
>
> *These naturally occurring antibodies are mainly IgM immunoglobulins. They attack and rapidly destroy red cells.*
>
> Anti-A attacks red cells of group A (or AB)
> Anti-B attacks red cells of group B (or AB)

ABO incompatible red cell transfusion

If red cells of the wrong group are transfused, in particular if group A red cells are infused into a recipient who is group O, the recipient's anti-A antibodies bind to the transfused cells. This activates the complement pathways, which damage the red cell membranes, and lyses the red cells. Haemoglobin released from the damaged red cells is toxic to the kidneys while the fragments of ruptured cell membrane activate the blood-clotting pathways. The patient suffers acute renal failure and disseminated intravascular coagulation (DIC). See diagnosis and management of severe acute transfusion reactions, page 92.

> ## Ensure the right blood is transfused.
> It is *essential* to ensure that no ABO incompatible red cell transfusion is ever given. This accident is likely to kill or harm the patient and it is *avoidable*.

The procedures described below have evolved over years of clinical and laboratory experience to minimise the risk of this disastrous error. These procedures will continue to evolve as better computerised systems are introduced to help staff to avoid errors in blood administration.

Rhesus D (Rh D) antigen and antibody

In a Caucasian population, about 15% will lack this antigen, and are termed Rh D negative. The remainder possess it, and are Rh D positive. Antibodies to Rh D antigen occur only in individuals who are Rh D negative, and as consequence of transfusion or pregnancy (page 87). Even small amounts of Rh D positive cells entering the circulation of an Rh D negative person can stimulate the production of antibodies to Rh D. These are usually IgG immunoglobulins.

The clinical importance of this becomes very obvious if a woman who is Rh D negative has anti-Rh D antibody during pregnancy. The IgG antibodies cross the placenta. If the fetus is Rh D positive the antibodies destroy the fetal red cells. This will cause haemolytic disease of the newborn. Without effective management, severe anaemia and hyperbilirubinaemia can develop and may result in severe, permanent neurological damage or the baby's death (see page 87).

Other blood cell antigen-antibody systems

There are numerous other antigen systems expressed on red cells, white cells and platelets. Transfusion can cause antibodies to develop in the recipient. Some of these antibodies can also cause transfusion reactions or damage the fetus. It is essential to detect potentially harmful antibodies in a patient before transfusion and where possible to select red cell units that will not react with them.

5
Pre-transfusion and transfusion procedures

Inform the patient (or relative)

See page 117

Explain the proposed transfusion treatment to the patient (or to the responsible person, if the patient cannot communicate), and record in the case notes that you have done so. They may be worried about the risks of transfusion and may wish to know more about these and expected benefits, and alternatives. Special issues arise with Jehovah's Witness patients (page 125).

Record the reason for transfusion

Before blood products are administered, the reason for transfusion (which should usually comply with local or national guidelines) should be written in the patient's case notes. This is important. If the patient has a problem later on that could be related to transfusion, the records should show who ordered the products and why.

Patients often do not remember information given to them. The prescriber's signed note in the case file, recording the fact that the patient has been given information and that his or her questions have been answered, may be as important in a medico-legal case as the patient's signature on a consent form.

Page 117 shows a sample information leaflet for patients. A new NHS leaflet is also available from hospital blood banks. Answers to many other questions that patients may ask should be found in this handbook. You should check whether your hospital has a patient information leaflet or uses the NHS leaflet *Receiving a Blood Transfusion* and if your patients receive it.

Ordering and prescribing blood components for transfusion

This section may seem to be very pedantic but experience in the UK and in other countries shows that

> **Dangerous or fatal transfusion errors are usually caused by failing to keep to the standard procedures.**

Acute haemolytic transfusion reactions are caused by transfusing red cells that are incompatible with the patient's ABO type (page 23). These reactions can be fatal. They often result from mistakes in identifying the patient when samples are taken, when blood packs are being collected from the refrigerator prior to transfusion, or at the time the infusion is started.

> **When ordering and giving blood products it is essential to follow the local procedures.**

It is a medical responsibility to prescribe blood components or blood products (i.e., to give the authority to administer). Completion of the request form may be delegated to a nurse or midwife. The responsibility for taking blood samples for compatibility testing may be delegated to a nurse or midwife or to a phlebotomist who has been trained to take blood for pre-transfusion testing.

Patient identification and blood samples for compatibility testing

Patients who may need transfusion must have a patient identification number, such as a hospital number, NHS number, or emergency admission number.

Any patient having a sample taken for pre-transfusion testing should have an identification wristband attached throughout the admission bearing the patient's surname, first name, date of birth, gender and identification (ID) number. For patients who cannot identify themselves, the wrist band should record (at least) the patient's identification number and gender. If the ID band has to be removed, it is the responsibility of the person removing it to replace it somewhere else.

Before you take the pre-transfusion sample from:
A patient who can communicate adequately:

- ask the patient to state surname, first name, and date of birth
- confirm this matches the ID on the wristband and the details on the request form

A patient who cannot communicate:

- take identification information from the wristband.

Label the sample tube *at the patient's bedside after the blood sample has been taken.* (Preprinted 'addressograph' labels are not recommended on sample tubes. If there is an established computer-based system, follow the local procedures for its use.)

Complete these details on the request form:

Patient information:
- ID (surname, first name, gender, date of birth and patient identification number)
- blood group, if known
- previous transfusions, pregnancies, reported red cell antibodies
- reason for the request
- which blood components are required
- any special requirements (e.g., red cell phenotype, gamma irradiated, CMV negative)
- how much
- when it is needed
- where it is needed.

If the patient is to get 'the right blood at the right time', you MUST make it absolutely clear to the blood bank when the blood is needed, especially in an emergency, and, if the blood is to be delivered, precisely where it is to go.

The hospital blood bank should not accept a request for compatibility testing if the request form or the sample is inadequately identified. At least 5% of samples arrive with labelling or form-filling errors. This wastes time and can contribute to serious errors or delays in providing blood. Time can be saved if the request form shows who to contact if such a problem arises and how, eg; their pager number.

Emergencies

Hospital units and the blood bank should have a jointly agreed policy for dealing with major haemorrhage. *Make yourself familiar with it.*

Tell the hospital blood bank *how quickly* the blood is needed for each patient. This allows the laboratory to choose the best method to provide the blood when it is needed.

Make sure that you, the hospital blood bank staff and the porters know:
- *who* is going to get the blood to the patient
- *where* the patient will be when the blood is ready.

The minimum identification for an unconscious patient is the identification number and the gender.

Pre-transfusion procedures – to ensure donation and patient are compatible

Type and screen (also called 'group and hold' or 'group and save')

The patient's blood sample is tested:
- to determine the ABO and Rh D type
- to detect red cell antibodies in addition to anti-A or anti-B that could haemolyse transfused red cells.

The patient's sample is held in the laboratory, usually for 7 days. If no antibodies are present, the hospital blood bank should be able to have blood available for collection in 15 minutes.

Red cell compatibility testing (crossmatching)

The patient's blood is tested:
- to determine the ABO and Rh D type
- to detect red cell antibodies that could haemolyse transfused red cells

- to confirm compatibility with each of the units of red cells to be transfused.

'Computer crossmatch'

Red cell units can be quickly issued for a patient with no further testing if:
- the patient's ABO and Rh type have been tested and also confirmed on a second sample (or on one sample tested twice using an automated laboratory system with positive sample identification).
- the patient has no irregular red cell antibodies.
- blood group results on the current sample and any historical record are identical.
- the identification of the patient and his/her sample is fully reliable.

Blood ordering for planned procedures

Surgical blood ordering schedule for red cells

Many operations rarely need transfusion so there is no need to crossmatch blood as a routine.
The type and screen procedure should be used for procedures where transfusion is rarely required.

For procedures that often need transfusion, a surgical team should have and adhere to a standard blood order that reflects the actual use of blood for patients having that operation in their unit. The request form must therefore show the procedure to be undertaken.

Further red cell transfusion

A fresh sample should be sent to repeat the tests for antibodies if the patient has had a recent red cell transfusion (completed more than 72 hours previously) as new antibodies may be stimulated, or weak red cell antibodies boosted, after the transfusion.

Compatibility problems

When the patient's sample is found to contain red cell antibodies that are likely to cause a clinical problem, further tests are needed to identify the antibody so that red cell units of a suitable blood type can be provided. The hospital blood bank will endeavour to provide blood that is compatible to avoid the risks of haemolytic transfusion reaction. The extra tests required will probably delay the availability of red cells for transfusion. When this occurs, *non-urgent* transfusions and surgery should be delayed until suitable red cell units are found, to avoid risks to the patient.

If the patient needs transfusion urgently the doctor on duty for the hospital blood bank should be asked to advise on the severity of risk if a red cell unit is given that is not fully compatible. This risk must be balanced with the risk of delaying transfusion.

Storage and collection of red cells for transfusion

Red cells must be stored in a designated refrigerator. It is usually the responsibility of the hospital blood bank to maintain these refrigerators and to specify the procedures to be followed when removing red cell units from them. Units of red cells for transfusion may be held within the hospital blood bank or delivered to another blood refrigerator to await collection.

Mistakes – collecting the wrong blood from refrigeration – are one of the commonest causes of patients receiving wrong transfusions.

The written procedure for removing red cell units for a patient should state:

- *who* is authorised to collect red cell units from the refrigerator
- *what* details must be checked against the labels of the units being collected
- *what* must be recorded about collection and return of the units, including:
    - the identity of the patient for whom blood is collected
    - the unique donation number of the red cell unit

- the time of collection
- the name of the person collecting the unit and their designation i.e., porter, nurse, doctor
- the time of returning units to the refrigerator if they are not transfused.

- *what* must be checked and recorded when blood reaches the clinical area to ensure that the correct units have been delivered.

Red cell units will usually be collected by the hospital blood bank if they have not been used (usually within 48 hours of the time for which they were originally requested). Red cell packs *must* be kept in the blood refrigerator except when actually being checked and transfused.

Administering blood components and blood products

The local procedures for administering blood components and blood products should be defined by the Hospital Transfusion Committee. Procedures should be readily available to all staff who administer transfusions and all those staff must be trained in the procedures.

Identity checks

Follow local procedures for the checks to be undertaken and the staff who may perform them. The current UK guideline on blood administration recommends that one member of staff be responsible. There is no bar to having two people doing the checks, but the person who signs for them must be a registered nurse, midwife or doctor. The hospital blood bank should provide with the packs of blood component a report or prescription form stating the patient's full identity, the patient's ABO and Rh D group and the unique donation number and group of each pack supplied (Figure 3b). The compatibility label on each unit should show:

- surname of patient
- first name
- date of birth

- gender
- patient identification number
- location of patient
- patient's ABO and Rh D group
- unique donation number
- ABO and Rh D group of the unit
- time for which blood is requested.

Occasionally red cell units will be supplied that are of a different ABO group from the patient's but that are compatible (e.g., red cells of group A for a patient of group AB). In this event, usually due to shortage of a particular group, the hospital blood bank should inform the clinician responsible and also record the fact on the document that accompanies the blood units.

If there is any doubt about whether the blood group is correct, check with the blood bank.

Before starting the infusion, it is essential to make the following checks [Figure 3]. Do these at the patient's bedside, or wherever the patient is to be transfused. DO NOT do the checks at the nursing station or in a side room. Set up the transfusion as soon as the checks are completed.

- **Are the patient identification details identical on**
  - the patient's identity band?
  - the compatibility label on the blood pack?
  - the form sent with the blood from the blood bank?
- **Do these details match who the patient says he/she is?**
  Patients who can communicate must be asked to state their surname, first name and date of birth.
- **Are the ABO and Rh D group and donation number all identical on:**
  - the blood pack?
  - the compatibility label?
  - the form sent with the blood from the blood bank?
- **Do the details of the pack and form match any requirements** for special types of blood e.g., gamma-irradiated, CMV-seronegative etc.?

Figure 3a :
Check blood pack
against patient's
wristband:
  - Name
  - Date of birth
  - Hospital number

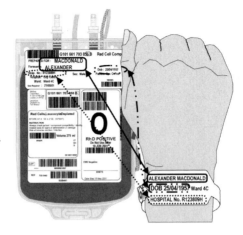

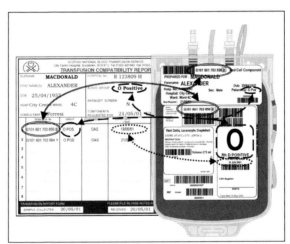

Figure 3b Check blood pack against blood bank form

If any discrepancies are found the unit must not be transfused (unless there is a signed report on the blood bank form, e.g; group B cells supplied for an AB patient and shown to be compatible). The hospital blood bank should be contacted. Generally it will be necessary to return the unit and the compatibility report form immediately to the hospital blood bank.

Inspection

- Check that the pack is in date and shows no signs of leakage, unusual colour or of haemolysis.
- Check that platelet packs do not show clumping or appear unusually cloudy, as this may be a sign of bacterial contamination.
- If a defect is suspected, contact the hospital blood bank for advice.
- If in doubt do not transfuse it!

Record keeping and observations

Transfusions should only be given where (and when) the patient can be observed by clinical staff.

The person administering blood must follow the hospital procedure for signing that the pre-transfusion checks have been done, and for recording the date and time for the start and completion of the transfusion of each pack. The compatibility form must be readily available during the transfusion. After the transfusion it must be fixed in the patient's permanent medical notes, together with the prescription sheet and nursing observations record.

In the patient's file, note the reason for the transfusion, what was given, and any adverse effects. A follow-up note should record the clinical response. Did the transfusion have the desired effect?

- Before starting transfusion record blood pressure, pulse and temperature.
- Check pulse and temperature 15 minutes after starting each pack.
- Observe the patient throughout the transfusion.
- Repeat blood pressure, pulse and temperature when the transfusion is completed.
- If the patient is conscious further recordings are only needed if the patient becomes unwell or has symptoms or signs of a reaction.
- An unconscious patient should have pulse and temperature checked at intervals during the transfusion.

Adverse reactions

It is very important to pay attention to any symptoms or signs – often occurring during the first 15 minutes of the infusion – such as distress, pain at or near the transfusion site, loin pain, backache, fever, flushing, or urticaria. These could be warnings of a serious reaction. A patient with a severe reaction can deteriorate rapidly, with hypotension, respiratory distress and collapse.

If you suspect a severe reaction stop the transfusion, keep the IV line open with saline, call for medical help and record the vital signs including blood pressure. Proceed as described on page 95.

Time limits for infusing blood components

Red cells

● Once a pack of red cells is out of refrigeration, there is a risk of bacterial proliferation.

● Do not take the pack from the refrigerator until you are ready to check and transfuse.

● If a red cell pack is out of the fridge (for up to 30 minutes), transfusion of the pack must be started immediately. If the infusion is not started within 30 minutes the pack must be returned to the blood bank and must be labelled to show 'out of fridge more than 30 mins'.

● From starting the infusion (puncturing the blood pack with the infusion set) to completion, infusion of the pack should take a maximum of 4 hours.

Platelets

● Never put platelets in the refrigerator.

● Start infusion as soon as the pack is received from the blood bank.

● Infuse over not more than 30 mins (or as instructed).

Plasma

- Once thawed, infusion should be completed within 4 hours.
- Start infusion as soon as the pack of thawed plasma is received from the blood bank.
- Anaphylactoid reaction may be more of a risk with rapid infusion.

Blood administration sets and equipment

Red cells, plasma and cryoprecipitate

Use a sterile blood administration set with a screen filter ('blood giving set'), primed with saline. It must be changed at least 12 hourly during red cell infusion. A new giving set should be used if another fluid is to be infused following the blood component.

Platelets

Use a sterile blood administration set or a platelet infusion set. A fresh set must be used for platelets.

Infants and small children

Use special paediatric blood giving sets. Use a screen filter if transfusion is given by syringe.

Cannulas

There are no special requirements for blood components.

Filtration

All blood components in the UK are leucocyte-depleted within 48 hours of the collection of blood to minimise the theoretical risk of transmission of vCJD. There is no additional benefit of bedside filtration of leucocyte-depleted blood components. It will have the detrimental effect of reducing the volume of blood component transfused.

Infusion pumps

Electronic infusion pumps may be used for blood components provided they are certified by the manufacturer as suitable for blood.

Blood warmers

Cold blood infused faster than 100 ml/minute has been reported to cause cardiac arrest. Keeping the patient warm is probably more important than warming the infused blood. The use of a blood warmer is often advised for:

- adults receiving infusion of blood at rates greater than 50 ml/kg/hour
- infants undergoing exchange transfusions
- transfusing a patient who has clinically significant cold agglutinins.

Blood warmers can be dangerous, as they expose blood to a temperature of 40°C. They must be correctly maintained and used strictly according to the instructions supplied.

> **Red cells and plasma exposed to temperatures over 40°C may cause severe transfusion reactions.** *Blood products must NOT be warmed by improvisations such as putting the pack into hot water, in a microwave, or on a radiator, as uncontrolled heating can damage the contents of the pack.*

Do not add other pharmaceuticals to blood products

No other infusion solutions or drugs should be added to any blood component. They may contain additives, such as calcium, which can cause citrated blood to clot. Dextrose solution (5%) can lyse red cells. Drugs should never be added to any blood product. If there is an adverse reaction it may be impossible to determine if this is due to the blood, to the medication that has been added or to an interaction of the two.

6

Clinical use of blood products

Surgery and intensive care

Principle: Minimise the need for donor blood products

- Transfusion carries risks; some of these are specifically due to the use of allogeneic blood (i.e., blood from another person). Autologous blood also has some risks

- Good clinical practice demands that any blood product should only be given when the patient is judged likely to benefit (i.e., the transfusion will do more good than harm)

- Prescribing decisions should be based on the best available clinical guidelines, modified according to individual patient needs. The reasons for giving blood should be written in the notes

- The need for transfusion can in some cases be reduced by stimulating red cell production with erythropoietin, or by using drugs such as aprotinin to reduce surgical bleeding. In some situations the need for donor blood can be reduced by retransfusing the patient's own shed blood (blood salvage)

- For some patients in some clinical situations it is preferable to use the patient's own blood that has been collected in advance of planned surgery (autologous transfusion)

- Modifications of routine practice can minimise the need to transfuse red cells, for example:

  - Checking for and correcting anaemia before planned surgery

  - Stopping anti-coagulants and antiplatelet drugs before planned surgery

  - Minimising the amount of blood taken for laboratory samples

  - Using a simple protocol to guide when haemoglobin should be checked and when red cells should be transfused.

Anaemia, bleeding and transfusion in patients undergoing planned surgery:

When should a red cell transfusion be given?

Conservative use of red cell replacement is appropriate in fit patients, especially the young, who are usually very tolerant of haemodilution and for whom it is especially important to avoid any long-term complications of transfusion.

In contrast, there is little clinical evidence to commend extreme measures to avoid red cell transfusion in elderly patients, especially if they have evidence of cardiovascular or respiratory disease.

In the past, surgeons and anaesthetists often used a simple rule: that a patient whose haemoglobin is below 100g/l (haematocrit <30%) needs red cell transfusion. This rule will certainly lead to some patients receiving transfusions that they do not need.

A recent large randomised clinical trial in critically ill patients demonstrated that a restrictive transfusion policy aimed to maintain Hb in the range 70-90 g/l was at least equivalent, and possibly superior, to a liberal policy maintaining Hb at 100-120g/l.

Further analysis of this trial suggests that the restrictive policy appears to be safe in most critically ill patients who have cardiovascular disease, with the possible exception of those with unstable angina or an acute myocardial infarction.

As a general guide, in normal healthy individuals, a transfusion threshold of 70g/l is appropriate and leaves some margin of safety over the critical level of 40-50g/l. At this level, oxygen consumption begins to be limited by the amount that the circulation can supply (see page 46). In older patients or those with indications of cardiac disease, the evidence available suggests that as a general guide it may be safer to maintain the Hb above 90 g/l.

Threshold and target haemoglobin levels for red cell transfusion

Practice must be based on transfusion thresholds and targets that are set by local guidelines as only in this way can important local factors be taken into account.

> **Where the patient is stable, is not bleeding and further major bleeding is not anticipated:**
>
> ● **Patients without cardiovascular disease and especially younger patients**
> > transfusion is likely to be appropriate to maintain haemoglobin levels in the range 70-90 g/l,
> > transfusion is unlikely to be appropriate at haemoglobin levels above 90 g/l.
> ● **Patients known to have or likely to have cardiovascular disease**
> > transfusion is likely to be appropriate to maintain haemoglobin in the range 90-100g/l.
>
> **If it is decided to maintain the patient's Hb in a different range, on clinical grounds, it is wise to record the reasons in the patient's notes.**

Preoperative requests for blood

These should be based on the local blood-ordering schedule. If the preoperative request differs from the schedule, the reason should be stated on the blood request. If it is not, the blood bank is entitled to query the order.

Intraoperative transfusion

Decisions generally rest with the anaesthetist who will take account of many factors including recorded blood loss and anticipated further losses.

Postoperative transfusion

The general guidance above applies. Postoperative blood loss must be monitored and there should be a clear protocol or individual management plan including the criteria for giving a transfusion, for charting blood loss and for surgical re-exploration if blood loss is excessive.

Simple steps to reduce the need for transfusion

Preoperative anaemia

Avoid sending an anaemic patient to theatre.

A patient who has anaemia before elective surgery is more likely to be transfused than a patient with a normal Hb. Patients being referred for elective surgery should have a full blood count done in time to detect and, if possible, to correct anaemia, for example by a 4-week course of oral iron. This alone will make a perioperative transfusion unnecessary for some patients. It is important to try to correct iron deficiency preoperatively, as in the period after a major procedure the bone marrow is relatively refractory to iron replacement therapy (similar to the anaemia of chronic disease).

Avoid haemostatic problems

Abnormal coagulation screen

If a patient admitted for elective surgery or an invasive procedure is found to have thrombocytopenia or an abnormal coagulation screen (prolonged PT or APPT) the procedure should be postponed while the cause of the abnormality is identified. If there is a known congenital bleeding disorder or one is suspected, the patient must be managed in conjunction with a Haemophilia Centre.

Low platelet count

If the platelet count is below $100 \times 10^9/l$ before starting a planned procedure likely to cause significant blood loss, or if the surgery is in a site where bleeding is specially hazardous, such as the CNS or neck, the cause of thrombocytopenia must be investigated before starting the procedure; this will determine further management. Before procedures such as lumbar puncture, insertion of lines, transbronchial or liver biopsy, or laparotomy, the platelet count should be raised to $50 \times 10^9/l$.

Warfarin

Unless it is contraindicated to do so, warfarin anticoagulation should be stopped before elective surgery for 1 or 2 days to allow the prothrombin time to normalise. A moderately prolonged prothrombin time should be corrected by giving vitamin K 0.5-2 mg IV, allowing 4-6 hours for correction.

Aspirin

Even a single dose of 150 mg (half a standard tablet) impairs platelet function for about 5 days. Aspirin should be stopped at least 7 days before planned surgery unless there is a specific reason for continuing it. Non steroidal anti-inflammatory drugs also impair platelet function.

Heparin

A specific anticoagulant management plan is essential for any patient on heparin who is to undergo surgery.

Special techniques to reduce the need to transfuse donor blood

Preoperative autologous blood donation

Some patients can donate their own blood - up to 4 units in advance of their own planned operation. It can be stored for up to 5 weeks using standard hospital bloodbank conditions. It must be tested, processed, labelled and stored to the same standard as donor blood. Before re-transfusion, autologous blood units must be ABO and Rh D grouped and compatibility checked.

Erythropoietin (page 57) is licensed in the UK for the purpose of increasing the amount of autologous blood that can be collected.

Patients suitable to predonate their own blood for surgery

- Operation scheduled is likely to need red cell transfusion
- Date for surgery fixed, so the blood does not become outdated
- Patient able to attend to have blood collected
- Patient's initial haemoglobin >100g/l (female), >110g/l (male)
- Sufficient time before surgery to donate at least 2 units of blood.

Own blood, compared with blood from the blood bank

- Autologous donations are often not used, either because not needed or due to procedural error
- Reduces (very small) risk of viral infection
- Reduces risk of developing antibodies to transfused red cells
- Does not exclude risk of receiving wrong blood due to errors
- Similar risk of bacterial contamination
- Iron replacement is required during autologous donations.

Autologous predonation with EPO (page 57)

- Accelerates recovery of haemoglobin after each autologous donation
- Adult can provide three to five units of blood over about 3 weeks

Procedure should be restricted to:
- Patients aged under 70 years
- Operations with a high blood loss such revision of a total hip replacement.

Not currently recommended in:
- Cardiac surgery patients (risk of thrombosis has not been excluded totally).

Intraoperative blood salvage

Blood aspirated from the operative field can be re-infused to the patient. Blood may be returned as collected, or it may be processed to remove plasma constituents. If large volumes of shed blood are returned without processing the patient may experience coagulation problems that could cause more bleeding. Blood salvage procedures have been evaluated by clinical trials in cardiac and orthopaedic surgery; systematic review of these studies indicates that salvage can reduce the proportion of patients who receive allogeneic red cell transfusion in orthopaedic surgery. In cardiac surgery, trials show only a slight reduction in transfusion of allogeneic red cells. This may be due to the inclusion of trials in which unprocessed blood was re-infused. Nevertheless, many clinicians believe, from clinical experience, that patients with major surgical blood losses do better if managed by re-infusing salvaged blood.

Postoperative blood salvage

Blood from wound drains can be collected and re-infused using special equipment. This procedure may reduce transfusion requirements in some operations such as knee replacement. The re-infusion of blood from wound drains may cause coagulation problems, so some authorities recommend that blood be processed by washing to remove plasma before it is re-infused. This requires more elaborate equipment.

Acute normovolaemic haemodilution (ANH)

There is controversy over the value of this procedure.
The anaesthetist withdraws several packs of the patient's blood, and replaces the volume with crystalloid or colloid. The patient's fresh blood that has been collected can be re-infused during or immediately after the operation. The blood must be taken into a clearly labelled blood pack containing a standard anticoagulant. It should remain with the patient until it is re-infused. Standard pre-transfusion checks should be done to ensure the correct pack(s) are re-infused. Re-infusion should be completed before the patient leaves the responsibility of the anaesthetist.

ANH is most likely to be of benefit where:
- anticipated blood loss is >1000 ml
- the patient's initial haematocrit is relatively high
- the patient can tolerate acute haemodilution to a low haematocrit.

Antifibrinolytic drugs

Cardiac surgery

Aprotinin and tranexamic acid have both been used to reduce blood loss in surgical patients. Aprotinin reduces allogeneic transfusion requirements in cardiac bypass surgery but some clinicians remain concerned about a possible effect on graft patency.

Aprotinin is often used in cardiac surgery where blood losses are predictably high (e.g., repeat operations to replace valves in patients with infective endocarditis).

Reviews of clinical trials indicate that tranexamic acid may have similar effectiveness. It is considerably cheaper, is a pure chemical rather than a bovine tissue extract, and is not associated with the risk of allergic reactions that can occur if a patient receives further aprotinin for a subsequent operation.

Cardiac surgery in patients on aspirin

Both aprotinin and desmopressin can reduce the antiplatelet effect of aspirin in cardiac surgery patients who require to continue aspirin until their operation.

Desmopressin has a particular role in the management of patients with milder forms of haemophilia and von Willebrand's disease. These patients, however, should only be treated at specialist haemophilia centres. (See page 59.)

Anaemia and transfusion in critical illness

Patients with critical illness frequently develop anaemia. Contributing factors to this anaemia are:
- frequent blood sampling for testing

- gastrointestinal blood loss (as a result of stress ulcers or erosions)
- occult blood loss (from intravascular lines, haemodialysis and haemofiltration circuits etc.)
- impaired erythropoietin production
- direct marrow suppression by cytokines induced by infection.

Patients with critical illness often develop shock and multiple organ failure due in part to an inadequate supply of oxygen to cells. Oxygen supply to organs depends on maintaining adequate cardiac output, haemoglobin concentration and haemoglobin saturation. These three factors determine the *oxygen delivery*. It used to be thought that survival could be improved by maintaining very high levels of oxygen delivery by transfusing red cells and giving drugs that increased cardiac output. This was called goal-directed therapy and a frequently used goal was a haemoglobin concentration >100g/l. It is now known that in most critically ill patients this level of haemoglobin concentration is not necessary. Most intensivists transfuse critically ill patients if their Hb falls below 80g/l and maintain the Hb concentration in the range 70-90g/l. A possible exception to this guideline is patients with known ischaemic heart disease. In this group, many intensivists prefer to maintain Hb in the range 90-100g/l. Most intensivists no longer aim to achieve a predetermined oxygen delivery, but assess whether the oxygen delivery is adequate in individual patients by examining urine output, skin temperature, and the severity of lactic acidosis.

Transfusion management of acute blood loss

This section refers to situations where rapid infusion of substantial volumes of fluid together with red cell replacement is likely to be required over a few hours, as a result of major bleeding. (*Obstetric bleeding:* see page 79; *gastrointestinal bleeding:* see page 53.)

General Guidance:

- Insert a large IV cannula, obtain blood samples
- Infuse crystalloid rapidly until an acceptable systolic blood pressure is restored (Notes 1 and 2)

- Manage other aspects of patient's condition (oxygen, maintain temperature, pain relief, etc.)
- Request coagulation screen
- Transfuse red cells to maintain adequate blood oxygen transport capacity
- Achieve surgical control of bleeding
- IV fluids should be warmed if large volumes are being given
- Pulse rate, systolic BP, pulse pressure, and urine output (catheter) should be regularly charted.

Notes

1. Systematic review of clinical trials of resuscitation in trauma reveal uncertainty about the best time to give fluid, and the volume of fluid to be given. While increasing fluids will help maintain blood pressure, it can also worsen bleeding by diluting clotting factors in the blood.

2. Some patients, e.g., those with ruptured aortic aneurysm or blunt chest trauma, do not benefit from full restoration of blood volume and blood pressure before surgical control of bleeding. Bleeding and coagulation problems may be worsened by aggressive fluid resuscitation in these particular groups of patients.

3. In severe head injuries, restoration of blood volume and pressure may reduce the extent of ischaemic brain damage.

4. Systematic reviews of clinical trials in humans have not demonstrated that the use of any colloid solution is superior to another, nor that use of colloid solutions is associated with better outcomes than with crystalloids in patients with trauma, burns or following surgery.

5. *See* Appendix 1 - Summary Guideline: Transfusion for major bleeding and Appendix 2 - Colloid infusion solutions.

Loss of blood volume	Replacement fluid
<20% up to 1 litre (adult)	crystalloid (e.g. 0.9% saline)
>20% more than 1 litre (adult)	red cells and crystalloid or colloid
1 blood volume or more	*See* page 110 Appendix 1
Blood volume estimate:	adult 70 ml/kg infant 80 ml/kg

Bleeding and transfusion: clinical and laboratory evidence of coagulopathy

Microvascular bleeding

This term describes a condition in which there is abnormal bleeding with oozing from tissues and puncture sites usually with at least one of:

● prolonged prothrombin time (PT) ratio >1.8
● fibrinogen <0.5 g/l
● platelet count < 50 x 10^9/l.

In a patient who has major bleeding, clotting problems usually result from:

● *dilution* due to replacement of more than one blood volume with plasma reduced red cells together with crystalloid or colloid fluids, and/or
● *consumption* of platelets and coagulation factors, provoked by tissue damage due to underperfusion, hypothermia or sepsis. This is a form of disseminated intravascular coagulation (DIC).

What can a coagulation screen tell you?
● Predict risk prior to an invasive procedure
    If PT and APTT <1.5 × normal and platelet count >100 (and no functional platelet defect), there is probably no significant increased risk of bleeding
● Help selection of products for management of a patient who is bleeding
    - PT/APTT >1.5   Give FFP
    - Platelets <50-100   Give platelets
                                (but see Table 11, page 64)
    - Fibrinogen <0.8-1.0 g/dl Give cryoprecipitate
● Help to diagnose the cause of abnormal coagulation other than that due to dilution (e.g., DIC, heparin, warfarin, acquired inhibitor, inherited deficiency)
● Help monitor replacement therapy

Use of blood components in the bleeding patient

Principle of replacement

When there is evidence, or the likelihood, of a coagulopathy *in a patient who is bleeding*, blood components should be given *before* the coagulopathy has become severe enough to make the bleeding worse.

Fresh frozen plasma (FFP)

When blood loss exceeds one blood volume (rapidly replaced with red cells and crystalloid/colloid) individual plasma clotting factor levels may fall to less than 30% of normal. A dilutional coagulopathy with a prolonged PTR >1.5 can be expected after replacement of one blood volume within 6 hours.

If the major source of bleeding has been controlled, and there is no microvascular bleeding, there is no need to give blood components.

If bleeding continues, the coagulopathy is likely to become worse, and FFP should be used.

The dosage of FFP should be guided by PT estimation, where practicable. If the laboratory result is likely to delayed, it is reasonable to give FFP after replacement of one blood volume while waiting for results. An initial dose of 15 ml/kg is conventional i.e., 4-5 units of FFP in an adult. Coagulation tests should be monitored if bleeding continues and it may be necessary to repeat the FFP transfusion.

Platelets

The platelet count is unlikely to fall below a critical level of $100 \times 10^9/l$ until more than 1.5 blood volumes have been replaced. If the platelet count falls below $50 \times 10^9/l$, or if it is falling rapidly towards that figure, and there is continuing haemorrhage, platelet transfusion is indicated. An initial adult dose of 250×10^9 may be provided either as a dose of pooled platelets or a dose of apheresis platelets.

The platelet count should be monitored if bleeding continues and further platelet transfusion may be needed.

Table 7: *Blood components in the bleeding patient: summary*

FFP: indications and dose for haemorrhage
More than 1 blood volume replaced or PTR >1.5
with continued blood loss
Dose: 15 ml/kg or 1 litre (4 packs) for adult of 60 kg

Platelets: indications and dose for haemorrhage
Platelet count below 50 x 10^9/l
Platelet count below 100 with continuing serious bleeding
Dose: 250 x 10^9 for adult

Cryoprecipitate: indications and dose for haemorrhage
Useful only if the fibrinogen is particularly low (<1g/l)
Early use of FFP may avoid the need for cryoprecipitate
Give 10 units initially and repeat based on fibrinogen estimation

Note: Cryoprecipitate is not available from all blood centres. 5 units of FFP (1250 ml) contains, typically, the same quantity of fibrinogen as 10 units of cryoprecipitate (approximately 150 ml)

Anticipated massive transfusion

In patients such as those with ruptured aortic aneurysms there is often a severe consumption coagulopathy in addition to the dilutional coagulopathy associated with fluid resuscitation.

It may be prudent practice to give FFP at an early stage to avoid the added complication of the development of dilutional coagulopathy. The risks and costs of FFP used in this way are small compared to the risk of death or major morbidity from the patient's presenting problems. Such use should be according to locally developed protocols that specify regular monitoring of the coagulation screen.

Other complications of large volume transfusions

Hypothermia

Hypothermia impairs haemostasis and shifts the Bohr curve to the left reducing red cell oxygen delivery to the tissues. Rapid transfusion of blood at 4°C can lower the core temperature by several degrees. The best safeguard is to keep the patient warm. A blood warmer should be used in adults receiving large volumes of blood at rates above 50 ml/kg/hr.

Hypocalcaemia

FFP or platelets contain citrate anticoagulant. (Red cells in additive solution contain only traces of citrate.) In theory, infused citrate could lower plasma ionised calcium levels but in practice rapid liver metabolism of citrate usually prevents this. However, in neonates and patients who are hypothermic, the combined effects of hypocalcaemia and hyperkalaemia may be cardiotoxic. If there is ECG or clinical evidence of hypocalcaemia, 5 ml of 10% calcium gluconate (for an adult) should be given by slow IV injection and if necessary repeated until the ECG is normal. It is very unusual for IV calcium to be needed during blood component transfusion.

Hyperkalaemia

The plasma or additive solution in a unit of red cells stored for 4-5 weeks may contain 5-10 mmol of potassium. In the presence of acidaemia and hypothermia this additional potassium can lead to cardiac arrest. This problem is best avoided by keeping the patient warm.

Acid base disturbances

Despite the lactic acid content of transfused blood (1-2 mmol/unit of red cells, 3-10 mmol/unit of whole blood), fluid resuscitation usually improves acidosis in a shocked patient. In practice, transfused citrate can contribute to metabolic alkalosis when large volumes of blood components are infused.

Adult respiratory distress syndrome (ARDS)

The risk is minimised if good perfusion and oxygenation are maintained and over-transfusion is avoided.

Where acute respiratory distress occurs during or just after transfusion of whole blood, plasma, platelets or red cells, the possibility of transfusion-related acute lung injury (TRALI) should be considered (see page 93, 98).

Acquired haemostatic disorders not associated with massive transfusion: disseminated intravascular coagulation (DIC)

Activation of coagulation and fibrinolytic systems consumes coagulation proteins, fibrinogen and platelets. Clinical presentation can range from major bleeding with or without thrombotic complications to a compensated state detectable only on laboratory testing.

Acute DIC

This is most likely to occur in patients with sepsis or due to an obstetric cause (see page 79). Haemorrhage due to obstetric DIC is usually only relieved by treating the underlying disorder but supportive treatment with platelets, FFP and cryoprecipitate is likely to be required and should be guided by laboratory tests. Acute DIC occurs in meningococcal septicaemia, and may result in thrombosis of large vessels in the extremities. Intensive therapy in an expert unit is essential.

Chronic DIC

This is usually associated with malignancy and may require heparin for treatment. Blood products should be used cautiously.

Transfusion for acute gastrointestinal bleeding

Gastrointestinal bleeding is a substantial cause of death in the UK. It occurs in 50-150/100,000 of the population each year. The mortality is reported as 11% among those admitted to hospital because of bleeding and 33% in patients who had GI bleeding while they were hospitalised for another reason. Blood replacement for patients with GI bleeding is summarised in Table 8. Special points in managing patients with bleeding from varices associated with chronic liver disease are given in Table 9.

Table 8: **Use of fluids and blood products in managing patients with acute gastrointestinal bleeding**

Severity	Clinical features	IV infusion	End point

Severe	• History of collapse and/or
	
	• Shock
	  – systolic BP <100 mm Hg
	  – pulse >100/min
		• Replace fluid rapidly
		
		• Ensure red cells are available quickly; use local emergency transfusion protocol
		• Transfuse red cells according to clinical assessment and Hb/HCT
			Maintain urine output >40 ml/hour and systolic BP >100 mm Hg. Maintain haemoglobin >9 g/dl

Significant	Resting pulse >100/min and/or haemoglobin <10 g/dl	Replacement fluid. Order compatible red cells (4 units)	Maintain haemoglobin >9 g/dl
Trivial	Pulse and haemoglobin normal	• Maintain intravenous access until diagnosis is clear • Send patient sample for red cell group and antibody screen	
No evidence of bleeding	May have 'coffee grounds' or altered blood in vomitus. Faecal occult blood negative		

Table 9: Replacing gastrointestinal blood loss in patients with chronic liver disease

Features	Transfusion Management	End Points
• Bleeding is often but not always from oesophageal varices and is often severe. Other causes such as peptic ulcer are not uncommon and must be excluded.	Insert one or two large bore cannulas. A central line may be indicated.	Systolic pressure >100 mm Hg. Haemoglobin 9 g/dl urine output >40 ml/hr.
• Bleeding from varices usually recurs if there is no intervention to control the varices or to reduce portal pressure. The prognosis depends on the severity of the liver disease.	Ensure red cells are available quickly use local emergency transfusion protocol: order 4-6 units.	CVP 0-5 mm Hg (not higher).
• Hepatic failure may follow variceal bleeding, but usually recovers if bleeding can be stopped and recurrence prevented.	Crystalloids should be used carefully. Saline should be avoided as sodium retention is usual and leads to ascites.	
• Thrombocytopenia is usual. The platelet count may fall below $50 \times 10^9/l$. Provided the platelet count is above $50 \times 10^9/l$, bleeding is unlikely to be controlled or prevented by platelet transfusion.	Platelet transfusion is rarely needed. If there is continued bleeding with a platelet count below $50 \times 10^9/l$, platelet transfusion may be considered in an effort to control variceal bleeding.	Platelet count may show little increment following platelet transfusion in patients with splenomegaly.
• Normal (i.e., pre-bleed) systolic BP is often lower than in non-cirrhotic patients.	Fresh frozen plasma is indicated only if there is documented coagulopathy e.g., INR >2.0.	Keep INR <2.0 if possible. Complete correction is rarely possible with FFP due to the large volume.
• Deficiency of coagulation factors except fibrinogen and factor VIII is frequent.		
• Giving red cells to try to raise Hb towards normal values may raise portal venous pressure, since blood volume is often increased. Over transfusion may contribute to rebleeding.		Coagulation factor concentrates may be indicated. Seek expert advice as some of the products have a risk of thrombogenicity, especially in patients with liver disease.
• Provided blood volume is replaced and cardio-respiratory function previously adequate, a haemoglobin of 9 g/dl appears to be adequate.	Transfuse red cells to approach but not exceed end point of 9 g/dl.	

Cardiopulmonary bypass

Cardiopulmonary bypass impairs haemostasis due in part to its effect on platelet function. In patients undergoing re-operations or in patients operated on with infective endocarditis, bleeding may be severe. It can be difficult to distinguish between surgical bleeding and impaired coagulation. Routine laboratory tests of coagulation do not accurately predict the clinical importance of the haemostatic defect and results may be too slow to aid clinical decisions. Rapidly available tests of coagulation, such as thromboelastograpy may help to decide on the need for blood component replacement.

Platelet transfusion is indicated if there is microvascular bleeding or if the bleeding cannot be corrected surgically after the patient is off bypass and once heparinisation has been reversed with an adequate dose of protamine sulphate.

Fresh frozen plasma and/or cryoprecipitate help to correct prolonged clotting times and may improve haemostasis. Routine use of fresh frozen plasma or platelets at the end of bypass has not been shown to reduce transfusion requirements.

Aprotinin (Trasylol) has antifibrinolytic and other effects on haemostasis and reduces transfusion requirements in cardiac surgery. In the UK it is generally used in specific situations such as bypass surgery in patients with infective endocarditis. Aprotinin is not generally used for first-time coronary artery bypass graft operations in adults. Tranexamic acid is an antifibrinolytic that appears to be as effective as aprotinin in reducing transfusion requirements in cardiac surgery.

Anaemia, erythropoietin and red cell transfusion in patients with renal disease

Anaemia affects 60-70% of patients with chronic renal failure (CRF). Many factors (iron deficiency, uraemia, hyperparathyroidism) contribute, but the principal cause is erythropoietin deficiency. Recombinant human erythropoietin (EPO) is licensed for use in dialysis and pre-dialysis patients.

Many patients with chronic renal failure have significant ischaemic heart disease. In these patients severe perioperative anaemia should be avoided. A haemoglobin level of 100g/l is a commonly used as a perioperative transfusion threshold for this group of patients.

EPO is administered twice or thrice weekly, intravenously or (more usually) subcutaneously. The principal side effect is impaired control of hypertension. Body iron stores are critical in maintaining the erythropoietic response. Parenteral iron saccharate can reduce the maintenance dose of EPO.

Immunological consequences of transfusion

Patients awaiting renal transplantation are exposed to particular risks by transfusion. Transfusion may stimulate broadly reactive antibodies against HLA class I antigens (allosensitisation) that increase the risk of renal allograft rejection and lead to poorer initial and long-term allograft survival. The principal risk factors for allosensitisation are the number of previous red cell transfusions, previous transplantation and pregnancy. Up to 30% of patients who have received 20 units of blood are allosensitised. Sustained high levels of broadly reactive antibodies are mainly due to repeated transfusion. The switch to universal use of leucocyte-depleted blood in the UK should reduce the risk of HLA alloimmunisation.

Use of EPO can almost eliminate the need for red cell transfusions. Several (but not all) studies show a decreased incidence of allosensitisation as well as a fall in antibody levels in sensitised patients.

> **Red cell transfusions should be avoided in patients on the renal transplant list other than for clinical emergencies.**

Before cyclosporin was used, blood transfusion was associated with a 15-20% increase in 1-year graft survival. With current immunosuppressive regimens this effect is difficult to discern. It is possible that planned transfusion, may still improve 1-year graft survival by up to 5% but only in patients with less well matched allografts.

Liver transplantation

Liver transplant patients often need substantial blood component support because of:

- large surgical blood losses
- preoperative coagulopathy due to liver disease
- intraoperative coagulopathy due to loss of liver function, massive transfusion, fibrinolysis, hypothermia and hypocalcaemia.

Liver transplant units have strict protocols developed with the blood bank to ensure that adequate blood products are available at the start of surgery and throughout the perioperative period. Intraoperative measures to reduce red cell requirements such as aprotinin and cell salvage are often used.

Patients with liver disease usually have a very high oxygen delivery to organs even if moderately anaemic. This is because the cardiac output is high as a result of systemic vasodilatation.

In most liver transplant units, red cell transfusions aim to keep the haemoglobin concentration at 80-100g/l during the perioperative period. An Hb level above 100g/l is usually avoided postoperatively, because higher blood viscosity may increase the risk of hepatic artery thrombosis. This is a principal cause of early liver graft failure.

7
Clinical use of blood products in medical conditions

Gastrointestinal bleeding - see page 53
Congenital haemostatic disorders
Haemophilia

Patients with haemophilia A, haemophilia B (Christmas disease), and von Willebrand's disease should be registered with and cared for by a haemophilia centre. This centre should be contacted when a patient with haemophilia presents to another clinical unit. Some patients receive recombinant products to minimise the risk of viral infection. Detailed guidance on the products recommended for management of these patients is published by the UK haemophilia directors and is regularly updated.

When a patient with haemophilia is seen away from a specialist centre, it is important to get the best help available, quickly (Table 10). This is particularly important where a head injury is suspected, as treatment is often required urgently.

Table 10: Initial care of a patient with haemophilia who has a bleed

Identification: if the patient is unconscious, check if there is information carried on a bracelet or medallion.

Contact: the haemophilia centre for advice and inform the local haematologist. It is very important to ascertain the appropriate therapy and whether an inhibitor is known to be present. If the patient has suffered head injury or other serious injury, coagulation factor replacement. should be started while these checks are being made.

Products for treatment: factor VIII and IX concentrates respectively are needed for haemophilia A and B. The nearest supply may be in the patient's home. In general, treatment should be with the product that the patient normally uses. In a real emergency and if clotting factor concentrates are unavailable, cryoprecipitate is the appropriate treatment for haemophilia A and fresh frozen plasma for haemophilia B.

Dosage: Factor VIII in a dose of 1 iu/kg should give an immediate 2% rise in plasma factor VIII. Factor IX (1 iu/kg) should give an immediate 1% rise in factor IX level.

Monitoring: Clotting factor levels are often needed to assess response to treatment. Contact the haematology department in your hospital or the haemophilia centre.

---

von Willebrand's disease (vWD)

The diagnosis and assessment of the treatment needs and response of vWD is not straightforward and requires measurement of the plasma levels of both factor VIII and von Willebrand factor plasma levels. For some procedures (and minor bleeding episodes) some patients can be managed with desmopressin (DDAVP) only. The patient's suitability for and response to DDAVP is routinely determined by the haemophilia centre where the patient is first assessed. If clotting factor replacement is needed, a factor VIII concentrate must be chosen that is effective for vWD. Cryoprecipitate was formerly the chosen replacement therapy but should now be used only if a virus-inactivated concentrate is not available.

> **Every effort must be made to obtain immediate specialist assistance in the management of patients with haemophilia or vWD.**

Transfusion in chronic anaemia

The mainstay of management should normally be the diagnosis of the cause of the anaemia, correction, if possible, of any precipitating factors e.g., blood loss, and appropriate replacement therapy with iron, vitamin B12 or folic acid. Anaemic patients are deficient in red cells but have a normal or increased blood volume. A rapid rise in haemoglobin is rarely required. In rare cases when red cell transfusion is felt to be needed, red cell concentrates should be used. Patients who are elderly or who have cardiovascular disease or megaloblastic anaemia are most at risk of developing cardiac failure from volume overload. Therefore red cells should be given slowly (4 hours per unit) and at a time when the patient can be observed. A diuretic, such as frusemide, should be given if there is a risk of circulatory overload.

Transfusion dependent anaemia

Regular red cell transfusion may be essential to manage symptomatic anaemia in patients with myelodysplastic syndromes, chronic lymphocytic leukaemia, aplastic anaemia or malignant infiltration of the bone marrow or inherited disorders of haemoglobin.

Inherited disorders of haemoglobin

The inheritance of thalassaemia major or sickle cell disease results in lifelong anaemia. These disorders require specialist investigation and management. In thalassaemia, there is a failure of production of globin chains that leads to red cell destruction and extra-medullary haemopoiesis. In sickle cell disorder, the production of abnormal sickle globin (HbS) is associated with crises (episodes of infarction and haemolysis) that are often related to infection. Replacement of HbS with normal adult haemoglobin (HbA) can improve these symptoms.

In *thalassaemia*, transfusion is the only currently available therapy. Treatment aims to relieve symptoms of severe chronic anaemia and to control skeletal deformity and other complications of the hypertrophic bone marrow.

In *sickle cell disease*, a variety of treatments including hydroxyurea and bone marrow transplant are under evaluation.

In all patients dependent on long-term red cell transfusion, special precautions are required to minimise the development of red cell alloantibodies, iron overload and non-haemolytic transfusion reactions (page 99). Susceptible patients should be vaccinated against hepatitis A and B before starting long-term transfusion. Preserving venous access is absolutely critical for these patients.

Anaemia in cancer

Anaemia is common during the course of malignant disease. Causes include:

- treatment-related marrow suppression
- bone marrow infiltration
- blood loss
- anaemia associated with chronic disease.

In the later stages of the illness, cachexia, vitamin deficiency and general malnutrition may also contribute to the development of anaemia. Anaemia is associated with a poor prognosis. The well-being of subjects with malignancy-associated anaemia may be improved by regular allogeneic red cell transfusion. This is often the mainstay of therapy in malignant conditions predominantly associated with marrow failure (such as myelodysplasia, myelofibrosis and aplastic anaemia) or extensive marrow infiltration (such as chronic lymphocytic leukaemia).

Specific haematinic supplementation may be of benefit in any patient in whom vitamin deficiency has been identified. Iron therapy is often poorly tolerated.

Erythropoietin (EPO)

In the anaemia associated with cancer, serum EPO levels are often increased, though they still remain inappropriately low for the degree of anaemia. EPO should be used according to local hospital protocols. It may benefit patients receiving myelosuppressive chemotherapy or radiotherapy, especially where the anaemia is poorly tolerated and in whom red cell transfusion would be expected to relieve symptoms.

Bone marrow failure and stem cell transplantation

Chemotherapy and radiation treatment of malignant haematological disease or solid tumours causes bone marrow suppression requiring transfusion support.

Transfusion may be complicated by graft-versus-host disease (GVHD), cytomegalovirus (CMV) infection or the development of antibodies to red cells or HLA antigens. The latter can cause febrile transfusion reactions and may reduce the clinical effectiveness of platelet transfusions, although the routine use of leucocyte-depleted blood is likely to reduce these complications. Patients who receive transplants of allogeneic haemopoietic stem cells may need special attention to selection of blood groups for transfusion (page 68).

Red cell transfusion

Red cells should be matched for ABO and Rh D type.

The local clinical management protocol should define the range within which patients' haemoglobin should be maintained A suggested (arbitrary) guide is to maintain Hb not less than 8.0 g/dl (PCV not less than 25%).

> In adults 1 unit of red cells raises Hb by 7-10 g/l. In children the number of mls of red cells to achieve a given increase in Hb can be estimated as:
> **(required increment in Hb g/dl) × 4 × (child's weight in kg)**

Platelet transfusion

Platelet concentrates (PCs) should be ABO and Rh D compatible wherever possible. ABO incompatibility can reduce the expected count increment (CI) by 10-30%.

Group O PCs are tested for high titre anti-A and anti-B and if positive should only be transfused to group O recipients. This is to avoid haemolysing the patient's red cells by anti-A or anti-B in the donor's plasma.

If Rh D positive platelets have to be given to an Rh D negative patient who may become pregnant in the future, anti-Rh (D) immunoglobulin (250 iu) should be given to avoid the 5% risk of the patient developing Rh D antibodies.

Table 11: Platelet transfusion

Thresholds for prophylactic platelet transfusion

- Stable patient $10 \times 10^9/l$

- To cover an invasive procedure e.g. central line insertion, the platelet count should be $50 \times 10^9/l$

- For invasive procedures in 'dangerous sites' e.g. CNS, raise the platelet count to $>100 \times 10^9/l$

Bleeding with thrombocytopenia

- Platelets should be transfused when there is clinical bleeding thought to be due to a low platelet count.

Adult dose

- $>240 \times 10^9$ (adult therapeutic dose, ATD) in a volume of 200-300 ml

- Infuse in less than 30 minutes

Dose for children less than 30 kg

- 10 ml/kg.

- Infuse at about 2-5 ml/kg/hr.

Monitor results of platelet transfusions

Platelet count the following day should rise by at least $20 \times 10^9/l$. If the increase is persistently $<20 \times 10^9/l$ this suggests refractoriness (see page 65). An alternative measure, the corrected

---

count increment (CCI) that takes account of the patient's size, may need to be used to determine whether a patient is refractory to platelets.

Patient refractory to platelet transfusions

Refractoriness is defined as a repeated failure to achieve a satisfactory increment after platelet transfusion. This may be due to the presence of antibodies to HLA. (About half the patients who are refractory have HLA antibodies and about half of these are refractory.) Other causes of an inadequate response to platelet transfusion include infection, fever, splenomegaly, DIC and treatment with some antifungals such as amphotericin and some antibiotics.

If the patient has anti-HLA antibodies and this is the likely cause of refractoriness:

- Try HLA-matched platelets collected by apheresis of HLA-typed donors.
- If the CCI is low following transfusion of HLA-matched PCs check for non-immune causes of refractoriness (fever, splenomegaly, DIC, amphotericin treatment) and test for antibodies to Human Platelet Antigens (HPA) if there is no obvious cause for non-immune refractoriness).

If refractoriness is due to non-immune causes and if there is significant bleeding, give two or three adult therapeutic doses (ATD) or give one ATD twice or three times daily.
If no cause for poor responses to HLA-matched platelet transfusions is found, and the patient is not bleeding, withhold prophylactic platelet transfusions.

Effects of transfused leucocytes

In the UK, all blood components are now leucodepleted to contain less than 5×10^6 leucocytes per pack. This is expected to reduce the incidence of complications such as alloimmunisation to HLA class I antigens and febrile transfusion reactions.

Removal of leucocytes to less than 5×10^6 per pack prevents HLA alloimmunisation in more than 97% of patients with haematological malignancies who have not been previously transfused with non-leucocyte-depleted blood or have never had a pregnancy. However, many patients still develop refractoriness. This is because in over 50% of cases it is a result of non-immune causes of platelet destruction, which include fever, splenomegaly, DIC and amphotericin therapy.

Transfusion-associated graft-versus-host disease (TA-GvHD): use of gamma-irradiated blood components

Transfused donor lymphocytes that are compatible with the recipient, but which recognise the recipient as foreign, can engraft and initiate TA-GvHD. Patients develop skin rash, diarrhoea and abnormal liver function and deteriorate, with bone marrow failure and death from infection usually within 2-3 weeks of transfusion.

TA-GvHD can be prevented by gamma irradiating cellular blood components to be transfused (25 Gy), since this inactivates the donor leucocytes.

Prevention of TA-GvHD

- All cellular blood components for bone marrow and stem cell transplant recipients should be irradiated from the time that conditioning therapy is started. It is recommended that autologous transplant recipients should receive irradiated blood for 3 months and allograft recipients for at least 6 months post transplant; some transplant centres recommend that allograft patients should receive irradiated blood indefinitely.
- HLA-matched platelet transfusions should be irradiated as should those from family members since HLA haplotype sharing has been shown to result in TA-GvHD even in immunocompetent patients.
- Irradiated components are also recommended indefinitely for patients who have received treatment with purine analogues (e.g., fludarabine) and in those with Hodgkin's disease, and patients with congenital cellular immunity deficiencies.
- All intra-uterine transfusions (IUTs) and exchange transfusions in the neonatal period should be irradiated.

(This is definitely required if the neonate received an intrauterine transfusion and is ideal for all other exchange transfusions if this does not lead to unacceptable delay in the provision of blood.) The same applies to top-up transfusions in neonates (if there has been an IUT or if the donor is a first or second degree relative).

- Granulocyte concentrates should be irradiated.

Patients requiring irradiated blood should be given an information leaflet and card available from blood centres informing them about their need for irradiated blood and that they should make clinical staff aware of this.

Prevention of cytomegalovirus (CMV) transmission

A proportion of stem cell transplant patients will be CMV seropositive pre-transplant and a number of strategies have been developed to prevent reactivation and clinical infection post transplant. All CMV seronegative patients with haematological and other disorders who are likely to receive an allogeneic stem cell transplant should be given blood components that have a minimal risk of causing CMV. Several studies show that the use of CMV seronegative components is associated with a less than 3% incidence of CMV infection or disease in susceptible individuals receiving autografts or allografts from CMV seronegative donors.

Indications for the use of CMV-seronegative blood components
- Transfusions in pregnancy
- Intra-uterine transfusions
- Transfusions to neonates and to infants in the first year of life
- Transfusions to the following groups of **CMV-seronegative** patients:-
    - After allogeneic bone marrow/peripheral blood progenitor cell transplants where the donor is also CMV-seronegative
    - After autologous bone marrow/peripheral blood progenitor cell transplants
    - Potential recipients of allogeneic bone marrow/peripheral blood progenitor cell transplants
    - Patients with HIV infection

Leucocyte removal also reduces risk of CMV transmission. It is not yet proven that this is equivalent to the use of CMV seronegative components.

There is no evidence that CMV-seronegative blood components are indicated when either patient or donor is CMV seropositive.

Transfusion support in stem cell transplant patients where there is donor/recipient ABO incompatibility

Approximately 15-25% of HLA-identical sibling donor/recipient pairs differ for ABO blood groups. The figure is higher in alternative donor transplants. ABO incompatibility does not affect either graft rejection or GvHD since ABO antigens are not expressed on primitive stem cell transplant.

Major ABO mismatch is defined as the presence in the recipient's plasma of anti-A, anti-B or anti-AB alloagglutinins reactive with the donor's red cells, e.g. donor group A and recipient group O.

Minor ABO mismatch is defined as the presence of anti-A, anti-B or anti-AB alloagglutinins in the donor's plasma reactive with the recipient's red cells, e.g., donor group O and recipient group A.

Major plus minor ABO mismatch is defined as the presence in both the donor's and recipient's plasma of anti-A, anti-B or anti-AB alloagglutinins reactive with recipient and donor cells respectively, e.g., donor group A and recipient group B.

Pre-transplant transfusion:
Recipient-type red cells and platelets should be given.

Post-transplant transfusion:
Use group O red cells, irrespective of ABO group until ABO antibodies to the donor ABO type are undetectable and the antiglobulin test is negative. Thereafter use red cells of the same group as the stem cell donor.

Use recipient type platelets until there is conversion to stem cell donor's ABO group and ABO antibodies to donor ABO type are undetectable. Thereafter give *donor type* platelets.

For FFP in the presence of a major or a minor mismatch, give recipient type FFP. For the situation of a major plus minor mismatch, give group AB.

Following graft rejection, revert to recipient-type red cells and platelets.

8
Clinical use of immunoglobulin products

Caution in the use of IV IgG

- Renal failure has occurred, usually in elderly patients, following administration of high doses of IV IgG. Rapid infusion increases the risk of anaphylactoid and other acute reactions
- The daily dose of 1g/kg must not be exceeded on any one day
- The maximum dose of 2g/kg must not be exceeded in a single course of treatment
- In the elderly a maximum dose of 0.4 g/kg daily over 5 days may be safer
- It is essential to adhere to the infusion rates specified in the package insert.

Immune cytopenias

Indications for IV IgG supported by clinical trials

Auto-immune thrombocytopenic purpura (AITP)

IV IgG in high doses has a role in the management of AITP in conjunction with steroids and splenectomy. IV IgG produces an increase in the platelet count for up to 3 weeks in about 70% of patients but it does not alter the natural course of the disease. It may be useful:

- to assist management of acute bleeding
- to cover surgery or delivery in patients with AITP if the low platelet count causes risk of haemorrhage.

A total dose of 1-2 g/kg divided over 1-5 days is usual in patients with chronic AITP. Further occasional doses of 0.4 g/kg may help to maintain an adequate platelet count.

Neonatal alloimmune thrombocytopenia (NAIT), neonatal thrombocytopenia due to maternal ITP, post transfusion purpura

IV IgG has been used in all these conditions with variable results. (See page 84 for NAIT.) IV IgG given to the neonate is effective in about 75% of NAIT cases, but any increase in the platelet count may be delayed for 24-48 hours or even longer. Much better management is to use compatible donor platelets, which can be combined within the administration of IV IgG. Many Blood Centres provide platelets from donors who are both HPA-1a and 5b negative (therefore compatible in 95% of cases of NAIT) for immediate use in suspected cases of NAIT.

High dose IV IgG given to the mother is being evaluated in the antenatal management of pregnancies in women with pregnancies previously affected by NAIT.

Severe thrombocytopenia is unusual in neonatal thrombocytopenia associated with maternal ITP in contrast to NAIT, and IV IgG is effective in some cases.

IV IgG is the treatment of choice in post transfusion purpura.

In all these conditions the initial dose should be 1-2 g/kg. Specialist advice is essential.

Antibody deficiency conditions

Primary hypogammagobulinaemia

These patients have an inherited deficiency in antibody production. Specialist advice should be sought, since they need lifelong replacement therapy to prevent or control infectious complications of immune deficiency.

Because intramuscular IgG is often poorly tolerated due to pain at the injection site (especially in children) it may be impossible to maintain levels of plasma IgG sufficient to prevent recurrent infection.

The treatment of choice is regular administration of IV IgG. The standard dose is 0.2 g/kg body weight every 3 weeks but the dose may require to be increased, or infusions given more frequently, if recurrent infections persist. It is usual to aim to keep the plasma IgG level within the range of normal values.

If IM IgG has to be used the conventional dose is 0.025-0.05 g/kg weekly. Subcutaneous administration may be suitable for some patients.

Haematological malignancies

Some patients with chronic lymphatic leukaemia or myeloma are unable to make effective antibodies and suffer from recurrent severe infections due to bacteria such as *Streptococcus pneumoniae*, *Haemophilus influenzae* that respond poorly to antibiotics. IV IgG at a dose of 0.2-0.4 g/kg every 3-4 weeks has been shown to reduce the frequency of episodes of these infections.

HIV

Some children with HIV who suffer from recurrent bacterial infections benefit from IV IgG, 0.2 g/kg body weight every 3 weeks. Episodes of infection, antibiotic use and hospitalisation can all be reduced.

Kawasaki disease

IV IgG is licensed for this condition.
A dose regime similar to that used in ITP is effective.
Indications for IV IgG in which there is a consensus that it may be helpful

Neuromuscular disorders

Treatment with IV IgG has been reported to be followed by clinical improvement in many other conditions.

Guillain-Barré disorder and myasthenia gravis

In these conditions IV IgG is a potential alternative to plasma exchange, but its effectiveness is not proven.

Indications not supported by clinical trial evidence

There is increasing use of IV IgG for conditions such as *chronic inflammatory demyelinating neuropathy* in which there is no satisfactory clinical trial evidence that it is effective. Use for such indications should generally be part of a controlled clinical trial or may be justified as a last-resort measure.

Plasma exchange

Therapeutic plasma exchange combined with other medical treatment contributes effectively to management of conditions shown below.

Indications for plasma exchange supported by clinical trials

- Guillain-Barré syndrome
- Chronic inflammatory demyelinating polyneuropathy (CIDP)
- Peripheral neuropathy associated with monoclonal gammopathy
- Thrombotic thrombocytopenic purpura
- Focal crescentic glomerulonephritis with systemic involvement (vasculitis)
- Rapidly progressive glomerulonephritis
- Wegener's vasculitis

Plasma exchange in conditions where there is a consensus that it may be helpful

- Goodpasture's syndrome
- Myasthenia gravis
- Hyperviscosity syndromes e.g., myeloma, Waldenström's macroglobulinaemia
- Cryoglobulinaemia
- Rheumatoid vasculitis
- Cutaneous vasculitis
- Persistent HELLP syndrome
- Familial hypercholesterolaemia.

Plasma exchange may be useful in other conditions such as pemphigus vulgaris, other autoimmune disorders, primary antiphospholipid syndrome, systemic vasculitis and cold agglutinin disease. Its use has been refuted by randomised trials in SLE and rheumatoid arthritis (without vasculitis).

In plasma exchange usually 40 ml/kg of plasma is removed. The replacement fluid is two-thirds human albumin solution and one-third normal saline, except in TTP (Thrombotic Thrombocytopaenic purpura) where FFP (standard or solvent-detergent treated) or cryosupernatant plasma are used. After extensive plasma exchange (three consecutive treatments) FFP (10-15 ml/kg) is given where there is a risk of bleeding due to depletion of clotting proteins, e.g. within 3 days of renal biopsy.

Intramuscular immunoglobulin for preventing infection

Normal human immunoglobulin and so called 'specific' immunoglobulin products (that contain higher levels of antibody against specific organisms) are used, often together with active immunisation, to protect against infection. A summary of the products and their use is given in Table 12. Practical clinical information about immunisation is given in the UK handbook *Immunisation Against Infectious Diseases* (Joint Committee on Vaccination and Immunisation for the Secretary of State for Social Services, the Secretary of State for Scotland and the Secretary of State for Wales, HMSO, 1996).

Table 12: The use of immunoglobulin preparations for prevention of infection

Immunoglobulin may interfere with development of active immunity from live virus vaccines. An interval of at least 3 months should elapse after an injection of immunoglobulin before subsequent MMR vaccination is attempted.

Infection	Indications	Preparations, vial content	Dose (Intramuscular)
Hepatitis A			
Hepatitis A vaccine is preferable to the use of immunoglobulin for prophylaxis of hepatitis A			
Tetanus	High risk injuries to non-immune subjects	**Tetanus immunoglobulin 250 iu**	250 or 500 iu
Use together with active (toxoid) immunisation in tetanus -prone wounds in the following: (i) unimmunised subjects, (ii) immunisation history unknown, (iii) over 10 years since last tetanus vaccine. Dose 250 iu but use 500 iu if more than 24 hours have elapsed since injury or if there is heavy contamination of the wound.			
Hepatitis B	Needle stab or mucosal exposure. Sexual exposure	**Hepatitis B immunoglobulin (HBIG) 500 iu**	500 iu
Administer immunoglobulin as soon as possible after exposure, with hepatitis B vaccine.			
Hepatitis B	Newborn babies of high risk mothers	**Hepatitis B immunoglobulin 100 iu**	200 iu
Administer immunoglobulin as soon as possible and with 48 hours after birth, with hepatitis B vaccine.			
Varicella zoster	Immunocompromised adult or neonatal contacts.	**Varicella zoster immunoglobulin (VZIG) 250 mg and 500 mg vials**	0-5 yrs 250 mg 6-10 yrs 500 mg 11-14 yrs 750 mg 15+ yrs 1000 mg.

Infection	Indications	Preparations, vial content	Dose (Intramuscular)
VZIG should be given to:	Immunosuppressed patients who within 3 months of the contact have been on high-dose steroids (e.g., 2mg/kg/day of prednisolone for more than a week).		
	Bone marrow transplant recipients.		
	Infants up to four weeks after birth:		
	• whose mothers develop chickenpox (but not zoster) in the period 7 days before to 1 month after delivery		
	• in contact with chickenpox or zoster and whose mothers have no history of chickenpox or who on testing have no antibody		
	• in contact with chickenpox and who are born before 30 weeks of gestation or weighing less than 1 kg; they may not possess maternal antibody despite a positive history in the mother.		
	Pregnant contacts of chickenpox without a definite history of chickenpox should be tested for VZ antibody before VZIG is given since about two-thirds of women have antibody despite a negative history of chickenpox. Those without antibody require VZIG.		
	HIV positive individuals with symptoms should be given VZIG after contact with chickenpox unless they are known to have VZ antibodies.		
Rabies	Bite or mucous membrane exposure to potentially rabid animals	**Human rabies immunoglobulin (HBIg) 500 iu**	20 iu/kg

Rabies immunoglobulin is used with rabies vaccine to provide rapid protection until the vaccine becomes effective. The recommended dose must not be exceeded and should be given at the same time as the vaccine. Half the dose should be infiltrated round the wound and the remainder given by deep intramuscular injection at a site separate from that used for rabies vaccine.

Infection	Indications	Preparations, vial content	Dose (Intramuscular)
Sources of Supply England and Wales		Normal Immunoglobulin: CDSC, Central Public Health Laboratory (CPHL) 0208 200 6868 and other Public Health Laboratories. Blood Products Laboratory 0208 258 2200	
		Tetanus Immunoglobulin: Regional Transfusion Centres.	
		Hepatitis B Immunoglobulin: Hepatitis Epidemiology Unit, CPHL and other Public Health Laboratories.	
		Rabies Immunoglobulin: Virus Reference Laboratory, CPHL.	
		Varicella Zoster Immunoglobulin: CDSC at CPHL.	
		All immunoglobulin products are supplied through the Regional Transfusion Centres	
Scotland		Protein Fractionation Centre, Ellen's Glen Road, Edinburgh EH17 7QT. 0131 536 5700	

Immunoglobulin products from commercial suppliers may be available through hospital pharmacies.

9
Obstetrics

Obstetric haemorrhage

Obstetric haemorrhage caused 12 out of the 134 direct maternal deaths in the UK in 1994-6. The blood flow to the placenta is 70 ml/min at term, so bleeding is likely to be rapid. It is often unexpected and difficult to control. Disseminated intravascular coagulation is common in obstetric haemorrhage due to placental abruption, amniotic fluid embolism and intrauterine death.

Haemorrhage due to obstetric DIC is usually relieved only by treating the underlying disorder, which usually involves rapid delivery. Supportive treatment with platelets, FFP and cryoprecipitate may be required and should be guided by laboratory tests. Bleeding into the uterine cavity, the uterine wall or the abdomen may conceal the extent of the blood loss. As a result, the patient may decompensate suddenly in the post-delivery period.

Successful outcome depends on:

- *routine* use of a management protocol with which all staff are familiar (Table 13)
- *clear* communication between the hospital transfusion laboratory and the labour ward
- *an agreed* code or form of words that will assist in the rapid provision of Group O Rh D negative blood (or blood of the patient's own ABO and Rh Group) and will avoid life-threatening delays due to inappropriate performance of a full crossmatch procedure in extreme cases
- *regular* 'fire drills' to familiarise all staff and to test the success of the protocol
- *training* and competence of the staff who transport samples and blood
- *effective* transfusion and haematology laboratory support.

A standing agreement between the haematologists and obstetricians over the issue of platelets, FFP and cryoprecipitate reduces the number of phone calls required and speeds response. Coagulation monitoring will help to assess the adequacy of the coagulation support and guide the selection of components but should not delay the initial issue of FFP or cryoprecipitate.

Table 13: Transfusion in obstetric haemorrhage

- Insert at least two large cannulas. Start saline infusion. Apply compression cuff to infusion pack. Monitor central venous pressure (CVP) and arterial pressure. Take samples for transfusion and coagulation screen. Order at least 6 units of red cells. Do not insist on crossmatched blood if transfusion is urgently needed.

- Warm the resuscitation fluids.

- Call extra staff, including consultant anaesthetist and obstetrician. Alert haematologist in transfusion department. Alert porters.

- Transfuse red cells as soon as possible. Until then:

    - crystalloid, maximum of 2 litres

    - colloid, maximum of 1.5 litres

- Give O Rh D Negative or uncrossmatched, 'own group' until crossmatched blood is available (see Appendix 1, page 110)

- Restore normovolaemia as priority, monitor red cell replacement with haematocrit or Hb

- Use coagulation screens to guide and monitor use of blood components

- If massive bleeding continues, give FFP 1 litre, cryoprecipitate 10 units while awaiting coagulation results.

- Monitor pulse rate, blood pressure, CVP, blood gases, acid-base status and urinary output (catheterised).

- Consider early transfer to ITU or HDU.

10
Transfusion of the newborn infant

Normal values

The blood volume is 80 ml/kg for a full term infant and about 100 ml/kg for a pre-term infant, depending on gestational age. At term the Hb concentration is 14-20g/dl with a platelet count of 150-400 × 10⁹/l. Sick pre-term infants can have a significantly reduced plasma volume which may expand following transfusion, thus reducing the expected rise in haemoglobin level. Results of coagulation assays can be slightly prolonged in full-term infants with more marked prolongation in the pre-term. Vitamin K-dependent coagulation factors are about 50% of the normal adult value at term while other factors, including fibrinogen, are in the normal adult range.

Table 14: Normal ranges for term and preterm infants			
	Term	Preterm (<37 weeks)	Adult
Haemoglobin g/l	140–200	125–200	115–180
Platelets x 10⁹/l	150–400	150–400	150–400
PT (sec)	12–17	14–22	12–14
APTT (sec)	25–45	35–50	25–40
TT (sec)	12–16	14–18	12–14
Fibrinogen g/l	1.5–3.0	1.5–3.0	1.75–4.5

Normal values for pre-term infants depend on gestation. Results of coagulation assays are technique-dependent and therefore results should be related to the laboratory's own normal range. The times given above are indicative only.

Red cell transfusion

Minimise blood loss
- Most red cell transfusions are given to replace blood drawn for monitoring.
- Micro-techniques, non-invasive monitoring and avoidance of unnecessary testing can significantly reduce transfusion needs.

For neonates, minimise donor exposure
- Neonates who may require several transfusions within a period of a few weeks should be allocated to a 'paedipack' system where one donation is divided into four or more small packs that can be used for sequential transfusions over the shelf life of the red cells (5 weeks). By this means, the number of donors whose blood is transfused to the neonate is minimised.

Use a local transfusion protocol
- Neonatal units that have a written local policy transfuse less than those without such a policy.
- In the absence of controlled clinical trials in this age group, recommendations for transfusion 'thresholds' are, at best, a consensus opinion against which neonatal units can compare their local practice.
- Table 15 may be a useful starting point for the preparation of local guidelines.

Table 15: Infants under 4 months of age	
Suggested transfusion thresholds for the administration of red cells	**Transfuse at**
• Anaemia in the first 24 hours	Hb <120 g/l
• Cumulative blood loss in 1 week, neonate requiring intensive care	10% blood volume lost
• Neonate receiving intensive care	Hb <120 g/l
• Acute blood loss	10% blood volume lost
• Chronic oxygen dependency	Hb <110 g/l
• Late anaemia, stable patient	Hb 70 g/l

Exchange transfusion

Exchange transfusion is generally carried out for hyperbilirubinaemia and/or anaemia, usually due to haemolytic disease of the newborn (HDN) or to prematurity.

- *For treating anaemia*, a single volume (80-100 ml/kg) exchange is generally adequate.
- *For management of hyperbilirubinaemia* a double volume exchange (160-200 ml/kg) is favoured.

Whole blood is often used but the haematocrit (HCT) of this product may be as low as 0.35 and therefore not optimal for an anaemic infant. Plasma-reduced blood with a HCT of around 0.5-0.6 is preferable.

- *Exchange transfusion* has a high incidence of adverse events. It should only be carried out under the supervision of experienced personnel.
- *Blood for exchange* transfusion should be irradiated (page 66).

Erythropoietin (EPO)

Recombinant human erythropoietin (EPO), when given with iron supplements, has been shown to reduce red cell transfusion requirements in neonates and is licensed for this purpose. However, the effect is relatively modest, with no real benefit in the first 2 weeks of life when sick infants are undergoing frequent blood sampling and are therefore most likely to require transfusion. The optimal timing, dose and nutritional support required to maximise the response has not yet been established.

Thrombocytopenia

The risk of bleeding is increased in preterm infants with platelet counts $<100 \times 10^9/l$.

Platelet transfusions are advised to maintain the platelet count as follows:

- $20 \times 10^9/l$ in otherwise well infants,
- $30 \times 10^9/l$ in infants with sepsis or other coagulopathy and
- $50 \times 10^9/l$ in the presence of bleeding.
- In infants with intracranial or other life-threatening bleeding to maintain the platelet count above $100 \times 10^9/l$. (Note this goal may be difficult to achieve in very sick babies with rapid consumption of platelets.)

Babies with neonatal alloimmune thrombocytopenia (see below) may bleed at higher platelet counts as the bound antibody interferes with platelet function. For this reason, some clinicians advise maintaining a minimum platelet count of $30 \times 10^9/l$ even in the absence of significant bleeding.

Neonatal alloimmune thrombocytopenia (NAIT)

This condition is the platelet equivalent of haemolytic disease of the newborn, affecting about 1 in 1100 pregnancies. Maternal IgG alloantibodies are formed against a platelet-specific alloantigen on fetal platelets inherited from the father. The commonest alloantibody causing NAIT is anti-HPA-1a in a mother who is homozygous for HPA-1b (80% of cases); the second commonest is anti-HPA-5b (15% of cases). The maternal antibodies cross the placenta and may cause destruction of fetal platelets and bleeding. Unlike haemolytic disease of the newborn, about 50% of cases occur in first pregnancies.

NAIT can give rise to life-threatening bleeding in utero or in the neonatal period. The most serious consequence is intracranial bleeding, which may lead to death, porencephalic cyst development or other forms of cerebral damage.

Advice from a haematologist about the management of NAIT should be sought as soon as possible.

Treatment of NAIT

- The condition is self-limiting, usually resolving within 2 weeks, but occasionally persisting for up to 6 weeks. Several transfusions of compatible platelets may be needed

- *Rapid treatment* is required if there is bleeding or a platelet count $< 30 \times 10^9/l$.

- *Give platelets* lacking the specific HPA antigen, either from a suitable volunteer donor (ideally both HPA-1a and 5b negative) or from the mother (*the latter must be irradiated*). Blood Centres should be able to obtain these platelets for use in suspected cases - there is no need to wait for laboratory confirmation of the diagnosis.

- *If maternal platelets are used they must be*:

  - *washed* to remove the alloantibodies and

  - *irradiated* to prevent transfusion-associated graft-versus-host disease.

- *If suitable platelets* are not available administration of high dose IV IgG (1-2g/kg body weight) is effective in about 75% of cases. IV IgG treatment can also reduce the period of dependence on compatible donor platelets.

- *Additional doses* of IV IgG may be needed 2-4 weeks after the initial response due to recurrence of thrombocytopenia.

11
Haemolytic disease of the newborn

Haemolytic disease of the newborn (HDN) occurs when the mother has IgG antibodies in her plasma that cross the placenta and bind to fetal red cells bearing the appropriate alloantigen. Red cells that have bound sufficient numbers of antibody molecules will then be destroyed in the fetal or neonatal reticuloendothelial system (extravascular haemolysis). This may lead to the development of anaemia in the fetus or neonate and neonatal hyperbilirubinaemia. In severe cases the fetus may die *in utero* because of heart failure due to the severe anaemia (*hydrops fetalis*). The neonate is also at risk of neurological damage due to the high bilirubin level.

> **Pregnancies that are potentially affected by HDN should be cared for by specialist teams with facilities for early diagnosis, intrauterine transfusion and support of high-dependency neonates.**

The mother may develop antibodies as a result of previous pregnancy during which fetal red cells bearing the paternal antigens have crossed the placenta and caused alloimmunisation. Alternatively, the antibodies may be due to previous transfusion. The fetus/neonate is not at risk unless it has inherited the relevant antigen from the father.

The most important cause of HDN is antibody to the Rh D antigen (anti-D). This antibody develops in Rh D negative women who have carried a Rh D positive fetus. It rarely affects the first pregnancy. Rather, this pregnancy acts as the sensitising event while subsequent pregnancies represent a secondary immunisation resulting in higher antibody levels. Smaller family sizes and the introduction of prophylaxis with Rh D immunoglobulin have reduced the incidence and severity of this condition.

Antibodies against other blood groups are now more common than anti-D but the majority do not cause significant haemolysis. Severe haemolysis or fetal anaemia may be found in cases affected by anti-c or anti-Kell and occasionally with other antibodies. ABO incompatibility between mother and fetus is common (e.g., mother group O, baby group A) and can give rise to a positive direct antiglobulin test and jaundice. Severe HDN due to maternal anti-A or anti-B is uncommon in Caucasians in the UK but is commoner in some other ethnic groups.

Screening for HDN in pregnancy

- At the time of booking (12-16 weeks) every pregnant woman should have a blood sample sent for determination of ABO and Rh D group and testing for IgG alloantibodies which may be directed against paternal blood group antigens.

- If an antibody is detected, the father's blood group should be determined to see if he carries the relevant antigen.

- The father may be shown to be:

  - Homozygous, in which case the fetus will carry the antigen, or
  - Heterozygous, in which case there is a 50% chance that the fetus will carry the antigen.
  - Not to carry the relevant antigen. This could occur for example if the antibody has developed as a result of previous transfusion or pregnancy with a different partner.

- Antenatal patients with anti-D, anti-c or anti-Kell (which carry the greatest risk of severe HDN) should have repeat testing regularly throughout the second trimester to monitor the concentration of the antibody.

- All other patients should be retested at 28-30 weeks (or up to 34 weeks for Rh D positive patients with no antibodies) as later development of antibodies or increase in antibody concentration may occur.

- If clinically significant antibodies are detected in pregnancy specialist advice should be requested to ensure optimal timing of subsequent testing and intervention.

Prevention of HDN: the use of Rh D immunoglobulin (anti-D)

Anti-D is an intramuscular or intravenous immunoglobulin with a high (quantitated) concentration of anti-D. It is prepared from plasma from donors who have become immunised as a result of previous exposure to Rh D-positive cells, often as a result of an immunisation programme. Anti-D is administered to Rh D-negative women who may have been exposed to Rh D-positive fetal red cells that have crossed the placenta and entered the maternal circulation. The anti-D destroys the Rh D-positive red cells and prevents active immunisation, thus preventing the production of Rh D antibodies.

Indications for anti-D immunoglobulin, in a mother who is Rh D negative

Fetal red cells may enter the mother's circulation as a result of:

- delivery of Rh D-positive infant
- therapeutic abortion
- threatened or spontaneous abortion
    - any after 12 weeks
    - any before 12 weeks that require instrumentation (e.g. dilatation and curettage)
    - any before 12 weeks if the bleeding is heavy or associated with abdominal pain
- invasive prenatal diagnosis
- other invasive intrauterine procedures
- antepartum haemorrhage (APH)
- external version
- closed abdominal injury (e.g., in road traffic accident)
- ectopic pregnancy
- intrauterine death.

Administration of anti-D

- Anti-D should be given as soon as possible after these events (within 72 hrs) if the woman is Rh D-negative and has not already developed anti-D.
- Prophylaxis is less effective if given later but may be of some value if given up to ten days after the event.
- 250 iu is given for events occurring before 20 weeks
- 500 iu (which will clear up to 4 ml of fetal red cells) is given after 20 weeks.

After 20 weeks any of these events should also be followed by a test that determines the volume of fetal red cells in the maternal circulation (a Kleihauer test or equivalent) as it may be necessary to give a bigger dose of anti-D if the fetal cell volume exceeds 4 ml. An additional 125 iu/ml of red cells will be required.

If there is repeated APH during the pregnancy, further doses of anti-D should be given at 6-weekly intervals.

Patients with potentially sensitising events may present to hospital accident and emergency departments or to their general practitioner. It is important that these staff are aware of the risks of sensitisation and carry out the necessary testing and administration of anti-D where appropriate.

Routine antenatal prophylaxis with anti-D

Despite the administration of anti-D prophylaxis, about 1.5% of at-risk mothers in the UK still develop anti-D. This is partly due to the spontaneous passage of fetal red cells across the placenta, particularly in the third trimester. The Royal College of Obstetricians and Gynaecologists has recently recommended that anti-D be given in the third trimester to all Rh D negative women who are not already sensitised. This matter is to be reassessed by the National Institute for Clinical Excellence (NICE) during 2001. Potentially sensitising events occurring around the time of routine prophylaxis still require to be managed with additional doses of anti-D and Kleihauer testing.

Management of HDN: refer early to a specialist unit

Patients with potentially severe HDN should be referred to a specialist fetal medicine unit for monitoring and management. The referral should be made before 20 weeks in those women who have had a previously severely affected baby, unless there is a new partner who is negative for the relevant antigen.
Affected neonates should be delivered in a centre which has access to specialist intensive therapy and experience in exchange transfusion.

12
Adverse effects of transfusion

Like other treatments blood can benefit or harm the patient. Good treatment decisions balance the likely benefit against the potential risks for each individual patient. Responsibility for the processes and decisions that make up good transfusion therapy are shared among the *manufacturers*, who must ensure the safety and efficacy of the product, *clinicians*, who must prescribe and use it correctly, as well as the *hospital blood bank* and those who are responsible for transport and communications.

Surveillance and reporting

Immediate reporting

All suspected transfusion reactions should be reported immediately to the hospital transfusion department. Immediate reporting is particularly important if an incorrect unit of blood has been infused in case blood packs have been transposed and another patient put at risk. The clinician should record the reaction prominently in the patient's case notes. Transfusion reactions should be reported to and reviewed by the Hospital Transfusion Committee

The Serious Hazards of Transfusion (SHOT) reporting system

SHOT is the United Kingdom confidential, voluntary reporting system for serious adverse events following transfusion of blood components and pre-deposit autologous donation and transfusion. Adverse events associated with licensed plasma derivatives or any other licensed blood product should be reported to the UK Medicines Control Agency using the Yellow Card. Incidents or 'near misses' should be reported initially to the consultant haematologist responsible for the hospital transfusion department who will report the case to SHOT.

Acute transfusion reactions

Acute, life-threatening complications of transfusion include:
- acute haemolytic transfusion reaction
- infusion of a bacterially contaminated unit
- transfusion-associated lung injury
- severe allergic reaction or anaphylaxis.

> **Serious or life threatening acute reactions are very rare. However, new symptoms or signs that arise during a transfusion must be taken seriously as they may be the first warnings of a serious reaction.**

Acute haemolytic transfusion reaction

Incompatible transfused red cells react with the patient's own anti-A or anti-B antibodies (see page 23). This reaction can destroy red cells in the circulation, initiate acute renal failure and cause disseminated intravascular coagulation (DIC). Infusion of ABO-incompatible blood is most commonly due to errors in taking or labelling the sample, collecting the wrong blood from the refrigerator or inadequate checking when the transfusion of the pack is being started.

If red cells are mistakenly administered to the wrong patient, the chance of ABO incompatibility is about 1 in 3. The reaction is usually most severe if Group A red cells are infused to a Group O patient. In a conscious patient, even a few ml, of ABO incompatible blood may cause symptoms within a few minutes (Table 16).

Infusion of the contents of a blood pack contaminated by bacteria

This is likely to cause a very severe acute reaction with rapid onset of hypotension, rigors and collapse.

Transfusion-related acute lung injury (TRALI)

Transfusion is followed by rapid onset of breathlessness and non-productive cough. The chest X-ray characteristically shows bilateral infiltrates often described as 'white out'. Treatment is that for adult respiratory distress syndrome from any cause. In TRALI, it is usually found that plasma of one of the donors contains antibodies that react strongly with the patient's leucocytes. The implicated donors are almost always parous women. It is very important to report TRALI to the blood service so that an implicated donor can be contacted and taken off the donor panel.

Fluid overload

When too much fluid is transfused or the transfusion is too rapid, acute left ventricular failure (LVF) may occur with dyspnoea, tachypnoea, non-productive cough, raised jugular venous pressure (JVP), basal lung crackles, hypotension and tachycardia. The transfusion should be stopped and standard medical treatment including diuretic and oxygen given.

Patients with chronic anaemia are usually normovolaemic or hypervolaemic and may have signs of cardiac failure before any fluid is infused. If such a patient must be transfused, each unit should be given slowly with diuretic (e.g., frusemide, 20 mg), and the patient closely observed. Restricting transfusion to one unit of RCC in each 12-hour period should reduce the risk of LVF. Volume overload is a special risk with 20% albumin solutions.

Severe allergic reaction or anaphylaxis

This is a rare but life-threatening complication usually occurring in the early part of a transfusion. More of a risk with blood components that contain large volumes of plasma, e.g. FFP or platelets. Signs consist of hypotension, bronchospasm, peri-orbital and laryngeal oedema, vomiting, erythema, urticaria and conjunctivitis. Symptoms include dyspnoea, chest pain, abdominal pain and nausea.

Anaphylaxis occurs when a patient who is pre-sensitised to an allergen producing IgE antibodies is re-exposed to the particular antigen. IgG antibodies to infused allergens can also cause severe reactions.

A few patients with severe IgA deficiency develop antibodies to IgA. Some of these patients have severe anaphylaxis if exposed to IgA by transfusion. If the patient who has had a reaction has to have further transfusion, it is essential to use saline-washed red cells or, if available, blood components from IgA-deficient donors.

Signs and symptoms of severe acute reactions

Table 16: Recognition of acute haemolytic transfusion reaction
Signs and symptoms may occur after only 5-10 ml transfusion of incompatible blood, so observe the patient carefully at the start of the transfusion of each blood unit.
If the patient has any of the following stop the transfusion and investigate.
Symptoms:
• Feeling of apprehension or 'something wrong'
• Agitation
• Flushing
• Pain at venepuncture site
• Pain in abdomen, flank or chest
Signs:
• Fever
• Hypotension
• Generalised oozing from wounds or puncture sites
• Haemoglobinaemia
• Haemoglobinuria
Fever is often due to a cause other than acute haemolysis. As an isolated finding, a rise of $1.5°C$ above baseline temperature should be investigated.
In unconscious patients only the signs will be evident.

Management of acute transfusion reactions

Since it may be impossible to identify immediately the cause of a severe reaction, the initial supportive management should generally cover all the possible causes. (See Figure 4.)

If the only feature is a rise in temperature of less than 1.5°C from baseline or an urticarial rash:

• recheck that the right blood is being transfused
• give paracetamol for fever
• give antihistamine for urticaria
• recommence the transfusion at a slower rate
• observe more frequently than routine practice.

If a severe acute reaction is suspected:

• stop the transfusion - keep the IV line open with saline
• call a doctor to see the patient urgently
• check and record patient's temperature, BP, pulse, respiratory rate
• check for respiratory signs - dyspnoea, tachypnoea, wheeze, cyanosis
• recheck the identity of patient and blood unit and documentation
• notify blood bank
• check blood gases or O_2 saturation
• provide further management according to the patient's developing clinical features.

Management of severe acute reaction

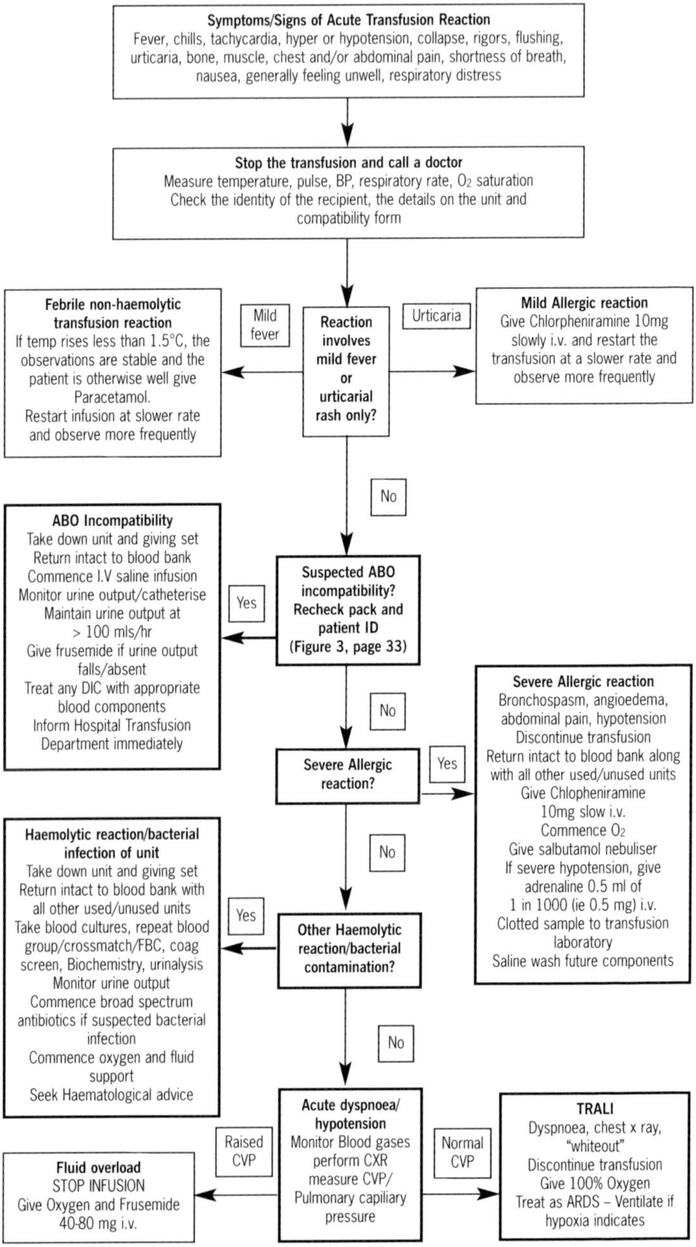

Symptoms/Signs of Acute Transfusion Reaction
Fever, chills, tachycardia, hyper or hypotension, collapse, rigors, flushing, urticaria, bone, muscle, chest and/or abdominal pain, shortness of breath, nausea, generally feeling unwell, respiratory distress

↓

Stop the transfusion and call a doctor
Measure temperature, pulse, BP, respiratory rate, O_2 saturation
Check the identity of the recipient, the details on the unit and compatibility form

↓

Reaction involves mild fever or urticarial rash only?

— Mild fever →
Febrile non-haemolytic transfusion reaction
If temp rises less than 1.5°C, the observations are stable and the patient is otherwise well give Paracetamol.
Restart infusion at slower rate and observe more frequently

— Urticaria →
Mild Allergic reaction
Give Chlorpheniramine 10mg slowly i.v. and restart the transfusion at a slower rate and observe more frequently

No ↓

Suspected ABO incompatibility?
Recheck pack and patient ID
(Figure 3, page 33)

— Yes →
ABO Incompatibility
Take down unit and giving set
Return intact to blood bank
Commence I.V saline infusion
Monitor urine output/catheterise
Maintain urine output at > 100 mls/hr
Give frusemide if urine output falls/absent
Treat any DIC with appropriate blood components
Inform Hospital Transfusion Department immediately

No ↓

Severe Allergic reaction?

— Yes →
Severe Allergic reaction
Bronchospasm, angioedema, abdominal pain, hypotension
Discontinue transfusion
Return intact to blood bank along with all other used/unused units
Give Chlorpheniramine 10mg slow i.v.
Commence O_2
Give salbutamol nebuliser
If severe hypotension, give adrenaline 0.5 ml of 1 in 1000 (ie 0.5 mg) i.v.
Clotted sample to transfusion laboratory
Saline wash future components

No ↓

Other Haemolytic reaction/bacterial contamination?

— Yes →
Haemolytic reaction/bacterial infection of unit
Take down unit and giving set
Return intact to blood bank with all other used/unused units
Take blood cultures, repeat blood group/crossmatch/FBC, coag screen, Biochemistry, urinalysis
Monitor urine output
Commence broad spectrum antibiotics if suspected bacterial infection
Commence oxygen and fluid support
Seek Haematological advice

No ↓

Acute dyspnoea/hypotension
Monitor Blood gases
perform CXR
measure CVP/Pulmonary capillary pressure

— Raised CVP →
Fluid overload
STOP INFUSION
Give Oxygen and Frusemide 40-80 mg i.v.

— Normal CVP →
TRALI
Dyspnoea, chest x ray, "whiteout"
Discontinue transfusion
Give 100% Oxygen
Treat as ARDS – Ventilate if hypoxia indicates

Fig 4. Response to a suspected acute transfusion reaction

Hypotension (systolic BP >20% below pretransfusion level)

In the absence of signs of acute fluid overload:
- resuscitate with saline 20-30 ml/kg over 5 mins
- monitor observations including urine output.

Sustained hypotension

In sustained hypotension:
- seek expert advice
- insert central venous line
- take blood cultures
- infuse more intravenous fluid ml to maintain CVP +5 cm to +10 cm
- decide on the need for:
    - IV hydrocortisone 100mg
    - broad spectrum antibiotics (see below)
    - adrenaline or other inotrope.

Antibiotics

- Seek expert advice if bacterial contamination is suspected
- Antibiotics should be chosen to cover gram-positives, including Staphylococcus aureus, and gram-negatives, e.g.:
    - a third generation cephalosporin, quinolones or aminoglycosides
    - plus azlocillin, ticarcillin, pipericillin.

DIC

- Seek expert advice.
- Transfuse platelets and/or FFP, guided by coagulation screen and presence or absence of bleeding.

If anaphylaxis or a severe allergic reaction is suspected

Give:
- high concentration oxygen
- chlorpheniramine 10-20 mg by slow IV injection over 1-2 minutes
- hydrocortisone 100-200 mg IV

- adrenaline 0.5-1 mg (0.5-1 ml of 1 in 1000) by IM injection; repeat every 10 minutes until improvement occurs
- salbutamol 2.5 to 5 mg by nebuliser.

If TRALI is suspected

- seek expert help
- high concentration oxygen
- IV fluids and inotropes, as for acute respiratory distress syndrome
- mechanical ventilatory support may be urgently needed.

If fluid overload is suspected

- frusemide 40 mg IV
- high concentration oxygen.

Note: It may be difficult to distinguish TRALI from fluid overload when respiratory distress develops during or shortly after transfusion. Raised CVP suggests fluid overload, while raised pulmonary wedge pressure suggests TRALI. Unlike other causes of ARDS, TRALI improves over 2-4 days in over 80% of cases provided there is adequate ITU management with respiratory support. The mortality was 20% in TRALI cases in the UK reported to SHOT.

Reactions due to red cell antibodies other than anti-A and anti-B

Intravascular haemolysis is normally associated with ABO incompatibility and only rarely with antibodies to other red cell antigens. Extravascular haemolysis occurs when red cells, coated with antibody and complement are destroyed by macrophages in the liver and spleen. This mechanism can remove as much as 400 ml of red cells from the circulation per day. The symptoms typically are fever and chills with elevated bilirubin and falling Hb. Antibodies with these properties occur against the ABO, S, Kell, Duffy and Kidd antigen systems. Antibodies against the Rh system antigens do not activate complement but antibody-coated red cells are nevertheless bound to, and destroyed by, macrophages.

This rare type of reaction usually occurs in patients who have developed red cell antibodies in the past, from transfusion or pregnancy. These may be undetectable when the patient is tested months or years later. However, a subsequent red cell transfusion can quickly boost the antibody. Antibodies of the Kidd (Jk) system are often the cause of such delayed haemolytic reactions.

A combination of the following features, occurring some days after red cell transfusion, suggests that the transfused red cells are being destroyed abnormally quickly:
- Hb falls more rapidly than expected after a red cell transfusion
- rise in Hb is less than expected
- rise in bilirubin
- positive direct antiglobulin test.

Febrile non haemolytic transfusion reactions (FNHTR)

Fever or rigors during red cell or platelet transfusion affect 1-2% of recipients, mainly multi-transfused or previously pregnant patients, although these reactions are probably less frequent with leucodepleted components. Features are fever (>1°C above baseline) usually with shivering and general discomfort occurring towards the end of the transfusion or up to 2 hours after it has been completed. Most febrile reactions can be managed by slowing or stopping the transfusion and giving an antipyretic e.g., paracetamol (not aspirin) (Table 17). These reactions are unpleasant but not life-threatening.

It is important to remember that fever or rigors could be the first warning of a severe acute reaction.

Allergic reactions

Urticaria and/or itching within minutes of starting a transfusion are quite common, particularly with components including large volumes of plasma e.g., platelet concentrates and FFP. Symptoms usually subside if the transfusion is slowed and antihistamine is given (e.g., chlorpheniramine 10 mg, by slow intravenous injection or intramuscular injection in patients who are not thrombocytopenic). The transfusion may be continued if there is no progression of symptoms after 30 minutes. Chlorpheniramine should be given before transfusion if the patient has previously experienced repeated allergic reactions (page 99). If signs and symptoms fail to respond to this, saline-washed blood components should be considered.

Delayed complications of transfusion

Graft-versus-host disease (GvHD). See page 66

> **Transfusion-associated graft-versus-host disease (TA-GvHD)**
> - **Leucocyte filtration does not offer protection.**
> - **The mortality is 75-90%.**
> - **Blood components from a parent or other close relative must be irradiated before transfusion to the recipient.**
> - **There is no effective treatment.**
> - **The condition is almost always fatal.**

Iron overload

Transfusion-dependent patients receiving red cells over a long period become overloaded with iron. Each unit of red cells contains 250 mg of iron and tissue accumulation can cause liver and cardiac damage. Chelation therapy with desferrioxamine is used to minimise accumulation of iron in patients likely to receive long-term transfusions

Uncharacterised effects on outcome: possible role of immune modulation by transfusion

Allogeneic blood transfusion alters the recipient's immune system in several ways. There has been concern that tumour recurrence rates and/or the incidence of postoperative infection could be increased in transfusion recipients. However, well designed clinical trials have not shown a difference in either of these outcomes in recipients of autologous or leucodepleted red cells when compared to recipients of allogeneic or non-leucodepleted red cells.

Recent randomised controlled trials (RCTs) have compared all-cause mortality in recipients of leucodepleted versus non-leucodepleted red cells or in patients managed to a high versus a lower Hb transfusion trigger level. These studies show some evidence of reduced mortality in certain subgroups of patients receiving either leucodepeleted blood or less blood overall. These observations are under investigation.

Table 17: Prevention of acute transfusion reactions

- **Febrile non haemolytic transfusion reactions (FNHTR)**

  If the patient has had two or more FNHTRs try:

  - paracetamol 1g orally 1 hour before transfusion
  - paracetamol 1g orally 3 hours after start of red cell transfusion
  - slow transfusion (RCC 4 hours, platelets up to 2 hours)
  - keep the patient warm.

  If the above measures fail, try saline washed red cells.

- **Mild allergic reactions**

  If the patient has one severe or two minor allergic reactions:

  - chlorpheniramine (Piriton) 8 mg orally 30 minutes before transfusion.

  If the above measures fail, try washed red cells or platelets resuspended in platelet additive solution.

- **Severe allergic reactions (anaphylaxis/anaphylactoid reactions)**

  Usually unpredictable.

  If the recipient is IgA deficient do not transfuse until you have obtained expert advice.

Post-transfusion purpura (PTP)

This is a rare but potentially lethal complication of transfusion of red cells or platelets. It is more often seen in female patients. It is caused by platelet-specific alloantibodies. Typically, 5-9 days after transfusion the patient develops an extremely low platelet count with bleeding.

Management

High-dose intravenous immunoglobulin (IVIgG) (2g/kg given over 2 or 5 days) is the current treatment of choice with responses in about 85% of cases; there is often a rapid and prompt increase in the platelet count. Steroids and plasma exchange were the preferred treatments before the availability of IVIgG, and plasma exchange, in particular, appeared to be effective in some, but not all, cases.

Platelet transfusions are usually ineffective in raising the platelet count, but may be needed in large doses to control severe bleeding in the acute phase, particularly in patients who have recently undergone surgery, before there has been a response to high-dose IVIgG. There is no evidence that platelet concentrates from HPA-1a negative platelets are more effective than those from random donors in the acute thrombocytopenic phase, and the dose of platelets may be more important than the platelet type of the donor platelets. There is no evidence to suggest that further transfusions in the acute phase prolong the duration or severity of thrombocytopenia.

13
Infections transmissible by transfusion

Over the past 30 years, the viruses that cause hepatitis B, AIDS and hepatitis C have been identified. In each case, effective tests were developed and rapidly introduced to detect and exclude blood donations that could transmit these infections to a recipient. The risk of being infected with any of these viruses as a result of a transfusion in the UK is now very low (Table 18, page 104). However, we must not forget that some patients who received transfusions before these tests were available have suffered very serious consequences of these infections. This is a constant reminder to avoid non-essential transfusions and to be on the alert for any other infection - perhaps previously unrecognised or unknown - that could be transmitted by transfusion.

Estimates of the risks of virus transmission by blood products in the UK

Plasma derivatives (virus inactivated)

There is minimal or zero risk of transmitting HIV, human T-cell leukaemia virus (HTLV), hepatitis B virus (HBV) or hepatitis C virus (HCV). Certain very small viruses that lack an outer lipid envelope are relatively resistant to inactivation procedures. If present in donor plasma they may not be fully inactivated in all current products.

Blood components

Plasma and cryoprecipitate may be subject to pathogen inactivation (Table 6). Cellular products are not currently subject to pathogen inactivation but processes for platelets are under trial.

The risk of HIV, hepatitis B and hepatitis C from transfusion has become extremely small. The current risk of a blood component transmitting HIV is less than 1 in 4 million, for hepatitis B is around 1/100,000 and for hepatitis C is less than 1/400,000 (for anti-HCV tested components and less than 1 in 1 million for components that have been tested for both anti-HCV and HCV RNA). Therefore, in the UK (where approximately 3.4 million components are issued each year) we expect to issue one component in every 1 to 2 years that could transmit HIV, around 34 components per year that could transmit hepatitis B, and - with increasing use of HCV RNA testing - substantially less than 8 per year for hepatitis C. A UK government expert committee has estimated for HTLV I/II that at most 3 recipients per year are placed at risk of developing some manifestation of HTLV disease during their lifetime.

The fact that a potentially infective component is released does not mean that a patient necessarily is infected. The actual number of infected recipients predicted is much less and very similar to the numbers that have been reported in the UK.

Bacteria can rarely contaminate a transfusion and may cause a serious reaction. Reducing such risks is currently a priority for action.

Table 18: Cases of transfusion - transmitted infection reported to SHOT 1996-2000 (September)

Year of transfusion	1996	1997	1998	1999	2000 (to end of September)	Total 1996-2000
HIV	1	0	0	0	0	1
Hepatitis B	1	1	1	2	0	5
Hepatitis C	1	1	0	0	0	2
Bacteria	1	3	4	4	3	15
HAV	1	0	0	0	0	1
Malaria	0	1	0	0	0	1

There are other infectious risks about which we are less certain because there is simply not enough scientific information available. In the UK, a great concern at the moment is vCJD, a human disease linked to BSE (so-called mad cow disease). There have been no reports of vCJD infection due to blood transfusion. Nevertheless, precautions have been introduced to try to reduce any possible risk.

Several recently described viruses such as GBV-C (so-called "hepatitis G"), TT virus and SEN-V have been shown to be transmissible by transfusion. None of these have been shown to be pathogenic. Human herpes virus 8 (HHV8), the causative agent of Kaposi's sarcoma, has so far not been shown to be transmitted by cellular blood components.

Hepatitis B

Tests for the surface antigen (HBsAg) are extremely effective. However there are very rare instances in which HbsAg may be undetectable in an individual who is infectious. An additional test may be introduced to further minimise the risk of transmission of hepatitis B by transfusion.

Hepatitis C

Serological tests to detect hepatitis C virus infection were introduced in 1991 and have been progressively improved since then: less than 1 in 400,000 blood components tested for HCV antibody could result in hepatitis C infection. The introduction of direct testing for hepatitis C RNA reduces the risk to less than 1 in a million. The infection is usually asymptomatic and revealed only by disturbed liver enzyme tests. About half the affected patients have chronic infection that can lead, after some years, to severe liver damage.

Other hepatitis viruses

There have been four reports of hepatitis A transmission by blood components in the UK over the past 25 years. Further viral processes are being introduced to inactivate protein-enveloped viruses such as hepatitis A in plasma fractions.

HTLV(I and II)

HTLV can cause tropical spastic paresis and a rare form of adult T-cell leukaemia. There is a latent period usually of many years between infection and development of illness. Only a small proportion of those infected become ill. HTLV I is transmissible by the cellular blood components, not plasma. The prevalence of infection is high in some parts of the world, notably Japan and the Caribbean. The link between HTLV II infection and disease is less clear, but infection is found in some intravenous drug users. Surveys in the UK indicate that the risk of HTLV-related disease following transfusion of blood is exceedingly low. Blood donors in the UK are not currently screened for HTLV I/II infection. However, leucodepletion may well be shown to reduce the risk.

Cytomegalovirus (CMV)

Approximately 50% of UK blood donors have antibody to CMV, but only a small proportion of antibody-positive donations transmit the virus through transfusion. Transfusion-transmitted CMV is of proven clinical importance in premature infants weighing less than 1200-1500 g who are born to CMV antibody-negative mothers and in CMV antibody-negative bone marrow allograft recipients who receive CMV seronegative grafts. Although the risk of clinical CMV infection is much smaller in recipient of autografts, some centres recommend that CMV-seronegative patients undergoing autografts also should receive CMV-negative products, For these patients CMV-safe blood components should be given. This is normally done by using donations that do not contain detectable antibody to CMV. CMV is only transmitted by leucocytes. There is evidence that the use of leucocyte-depleted blood components is effective in preventing transmission of CMV by transfusion. However, the use of CMV antibody-negative components, in addition to leucocyte-depletion, currently remains the treatment of choice in clinical situations where there is high risk of CMV transmission (see page 67). Fresh frozen plasma and cryoprecipitate do not transmit CMV.

Human parvovirus B19

This protein-enveloped virus may not be inactivated in all current plasma fractions. Processes are being introduced to do this. There is evidence that HPV B19 infection is associated with bone marrow suppression affecting red cell production in occasional patients.

Treponemal infections

All donations are screened for serological evidence of *Treponema pallidum* infection. A further safeguard is that infectivity of *T. pallidum* declines as blood is stored at 2-6°C. Transfusion transmission is estimated to occur with a frequency of about 1/40,000 in the USA. There have been no reports of transfusion transmission in the UK in recent years.

Other bacterial infections

Bacterial contamination of a blood component is a rare cause of very severe and often lethal transfusion reactions. In the UK, 16 incidents (4 fatalities) were identified during the 6 years to 2000, giving a rate of about 2/million units transfused. This is likely to be an underestimate. Bacteria associated with severe septic reactions to red cell transfusion are usually cold-growing strains. *Pseudomonas fluorescens*, the type most often isolated is an environmental contaminant. *Yersinia enterocolitica* is an example of an organism that may enter a blood donor pack that is collected from a donor during an episode of asymptomatic bacteraemia. Skin contaminants such as staphylococci may proliferate in platelet concentrates stored at 20-22°C and this is a factor limiting the safe storage life of platelet concentrates. Platelets are more likely to be associated with bacterial complications than are red cells. New methods for reducing this risk are in development.

Malaria

Donor selection procedures are designed to exclude potentially infectious individuals from donating red cells for transfusion. Transfusion-transmitted malaria occurs with a frequency of about 0.25/million units collected in the USA. Comparable data for the UK are not available. Only four cases of transfusion malaria (all due to *Plasmodium falciparum*) have been reported in the UK in the past 25 years. A screening test for donors has been evaluated that detects malarial antibody in potential blood donors who have a history of potential exposure to malarial infection. This test may enable some people who are currently excluded to be accepted as donors
.

Chagas disease

This is caused by *Trypanosoma cruzi* and is transmissible by transfusion. Four cases have been reported in the US, but none in the UK. It is an important problem in parts of South America where the infection is endemic. A new test for antibody can now allow the acceptance of donors at risk of infection who would previously have been excluded.

Appendix 1
Summary guideline: Transfusion for major bleeding

• Arrest bleeding • Contact key personnel	• Early surgical or obstetric intervention • Upper G/I tract procedures • Interventional radiology • Most appropriate surgical team • Duty anaesthetist • Blood bank	
• Restore circulating volume N.B. In patients with major vessel or cardiac injury, it may be appropriate to restrict volume replacement after discussion with surgical team	• Insert wide bore peripheral cannulas • Give adequate volumes of crystalloid/blood • Aim to maintain normal BP and urine output >30ml/hr in adults (or 0.5ml/kg/hour)	• Blood loss is often underestimated • Refer to local guidelines for the resuscitation of trauma patients and for red cell transfusion • Monitor CVP if haemodynamically unstable
• Request laboratory investigations	• FBC, PT, APTT, fibrinogen; blood bank sample, biochemical profile, blood gases • Ensure correct sample identity for transfusion samples • Repeat FBC, PT, APTT, fibrinogen every 4 hrs, or after 1/3 blood volume replacement, or after infusion of FFP	• Take samples at earliest opportunity as results may be affected by colloid infusion • Misidentification is commonest transfusion risk • May need to give FFP and platelets before the FBC and coagulation results available
• Request suitable red cells N.B. All red cells are now leucocyte-depleted. The volume is provided on each pack, and is in the range of 220-420ml.	• Blood needed immediately - use 'Emergency stock' group O Rh D neg • Blood needed in 15-60 minutes - uncrossmatched ABO group specific will be provided when blood group known (15-60 minutes from receipt	• Contact Blood Transfusion laboratory or oncall MLSO and provide relevant details • Collect sample for group and crossmatch before using emergency stock • Emergency use of Rh D pos blood is acceptable if patient is male or

	of sample in laboratory)
	• Blood needed in 60 minutes or longer – fully crossmatched blood will be provided	postmenopausal female) • Blood warmer indicated if large volumes are transfused rapidly • Consider use of cell salvage
• Consider the use of platelets	• Anticipate platelet count <50 x 10⁹ /l after 1.5-2 x blood volume replacement • Dose: 10ml/kg body weight for a neonate or small child, otherwise one 'adult therapeutic dose' (one pack)	• Target platelet count: >100 x 10⁹ /l for multiple/CNS trauma, >50 x 10⁹ /l for other situations • May need to use platelets before laboratory results available - take FBC sample before platelets transfused
• Consider the use of FFP	• Anticipate coagulation factor deficiency after blood loss of 1.5 x blood volume • Aim for PT and APTT <1.5 x mean control • Allow for 30 mins thawing time • Dose: 12-15 ml/kg body wt = 1 litre or 4 units for an adult	• PT/APTT >1.5 x mean control correlates with increased surgical bleeding • May need to use FFP before laboratory results available - take sample for PT, APTT, fibrinogen before FFP transfused
• Consider the use of cryoprecipitate	• To replace fibrinogen and FVIII • Aim for fibrinogen >1.0g/l • Allow for 30 mins thawing time • Dose: 1pack/10kg body wt	• Fibrinogen <0.5 strongly associated with microvascular bleeding
• Suspect DIC	• Treat underlying cause if possible	• Shock, hypothermia, acidosis – risk of DIC • Mortality of DIC is high

Appendix 2
Non plasma colloid volume expanders

Product	Source	Effects on haemostasis	Use in major haemorrhage	Comments on use in haemorrhage
				Systematic reviews of clinical trials indicate that there are no benefits from the use of colloid solutions for resuscitation. This conclusion remains the subject of controversy
Modified fluid gelatin (e.g., Gelofusine, Haemaccel)	Cattle bone gelatin Heat/chemical treated	No	No volume limitation	Bovine origin may concern some clinicians or patients
Pentastarch (e.g., Haes-steril, pentaspan)	Maize starch, chemically modified	Yes, mild	Use only up to volume stated in product information	Inhibition of clotting not reported to be a clinically significant disadvantage
Hetastarch (e.g., Hespan)	Maize starch, chemically modified	Yes	Use only up to volume stated in product information	Inhibition of clotting may be a clinically significant disadvantage
Dextran 70	Hydrolysed starch	Yes	Use only up to volume stated in product information	Inhibition of clotting may be a clinically significant disadvantage
Dextran 40	Hydrolysed starch	Yes	Not appropriate	Inhibition of clotting may be a clinically significant disadvantage

| Human albumin 4 or 5% | Processed human plasma | No | Yes | See Table 6, page 19 |
| Human albumin 20% | Processed human plasma | No | | Unsuitable |

Appendix 3
Information for patients

The risks of having a blood transfusion need to be balanced against the risks of not receiving one. Transfusion can save life and plays an essential part in the treatment of some conditions. Like other powerful therapies, it should only be used when it is really necessary.

At present in the United Kingdom formal informed consent is not required prior to a blood transfusion. However, it is good clinical practice to provide adequate information to the patient and to make sure that it is understood. It is suggested that discussion with the patient should include the information in the following outline for a patient information leaflet.

Blood Transfusion and You (A Patient's Guide)

Why might a blood transfusion be needed?

The two most common reasons for a blood transfusion are:
● to replace blood lost during an operation or after an accident, and
● to treat anaemia (lack of red blood cells).

It is expected that some blood will be lost during surgery. Small amounts can be replaced by solutions of salt or glucose or by the use of synthetic substances such as dextrans or gelatin. Larger amounts of lost blood will need to be replaced by blood transfusion to avoid the dangerous effects that you could suffer.

An accident can often lead to rapid loss of blood. In these circumstances, blood transfusion will be necessary to replace what has been lost.

Anaemia has a number of causes, but the effects are the same. Your body will not have enough red cells to carry the oxygen you need. As a result, you will feel tired and breathless. It is often possible to treat anaemia with medicines and vitamins but blood transfusion may be necessary.

What are the risks?

All blood transfused in the United Kingdom is collected from unpaid volunteers. Before they donate blood they are carefully selected to ensure they are in good health.

Following donation, each individual unit of blood is tested. Only blood that passes these tests is used for transfusion. The tests look for viruses that can be transmitted by blood. These are hepatitis B, hepatitis C and HIV – the virus that causes AIDS. As a result of these measures, the risk of being infected by these viruses through receiving a blood transfusion is extremely small. In the United Kingdom over the past 5 years during which nearly 8 million donation of blood were collected and used, there is 1 report of a patient being infected with HIV by transfusion, 5 with hepatitis B and 2 with hepatitis C.

In recent years there has been concern over the possible transmission of variant CJD, the human form of mad cow disease. We do not know about the risk of vCJD transmission by blood at present. As a precaution all blood used for transfusion in the United Kingdom has been treated to remove the white cells.

If you might need a transfusion, your blood will be tested to ensure that it is compatible with the the donated blood you may receive. This is necessary to make sure that your blood group fits as closely as possible to the transfused blood, but the match can never be perfect, as there are too many different blood groups to make this possible. Severe reactions due to mismatching are very rare. There is a confidential scheme (Serious Hazards of Transfusion, SHOT) which notes any reactions. These can then be investigated and, if possible, prevented in future.

What are the alternatives?

If you have previously been generally healthy, it may be possible to use your own blood (autologous transfusion). This is only useful for some operations. It may be possible to collect blood from you during the month before the operation, and transfuse it back to you during surgery. Alternatively, for some operations, the blood you lose during surgery can be collected and transfused back to you.

Over the years a great deal of research has been done to try to find a synthetic or chemical alternative to blood. These substances are on trial, and are not yet available for routine use.

What if I have other questions?

If you need more information, it is best to ask the nurses or doctors on the ward and to discuss with them your concerns.

> **Remember: A blood transfusion can be a lifesaving treatment. The risks of having a blood transfusion will be balanced against the risks to you of not receiving one.**

Appendix 4
Directed donation: yes or no ?

This information is provided for clinical staff, who may require to discuss this difficult question with patients and parents. The general policy of the UK transfusion services is to discourage directed donation, as the published evidence shows that there is a higher probability of transfusion-transmissible infectious agents among these donors than among conventional volunteers.

- Directed donation is the donation of blood, usually by a parent or family member, for a specific patient.
- Usually the request to provide or receive directed donation is from family members.
- Generally the motivation is concern about disease transmission.
- The assumption made by the donor, patient or parents is that there is a lower risk of disease transmission if the chosen person's blood is used than with blood from the blood bank.
- However the potential donor may be inhibited from giving frank answers to questions about risk factors for infections, so this blood is not necessarily as safe as that of voluntary donors.

Concerns about directed donations

It is essential to discuss the following potential problems with the individuals concerned.

Blood group compatibility

A donor must be of a compatible blood group (e.g., a patient who is group O can only receive group O blood).

Infection

The donor *must* fulfill all the criteria used to select normal volunteer donors. Any individual who is felt to be unfit to donate when the normal donor screening processes are carried out will not be accepted as a directed donor. Studies show that directed donors do not have a lower risk of infectious disease transmission (based on positive tests for hepatitis or HIV). In fact, in some studies there has been a higher incidence of markers of infection in those who want to be directed donors than in the normal donor population. This is especially a concern when the directed donor is a first-time donor rather than a regular blood donor, as there will be no information from previous testing.

Transfusion-associated graft-versus-host disease (TA-GvHD)

Donors who are first- or second-degree relatives of the patient have a relatively high likelihood of having a similar tissue type - brothers and sisters have a 1 in 4 chance of being a complete match, parents and children of the patient will be at least haploidentical, i.e., matched for 50% of the tissue type. Thus there is a risk of the recipient developing graft-versus-host disease which is a fatal condition (see page 66). For this reason

> **all donations from related donors must be irradiated before transfusion to kill any remaining white cells.**

Other Immunological Complications

There are additional concerns when a mother wishes to donate for her child. She should be aware that she may have antibodies to the baby's blood cells (red cells, white cells, platelets). Transfusion of her blood could cause the baby to suffer an acute or delayed transfusion reaction, respiratory problems or a low platelet count.

Transfusion of blood from a father to a young baby may also lead to a transfusion reaction as the baby may have maternal antibodies against the father's cells. This can result in haemolysis (breakdown of the father's red cells), or reactions to the father's white cells or platelets leading to fevers, breathing problems or drop in blood pressure etc as the baby's blood may contain antibodies passed from the mother *in utero* that can react with the father's cells. These antibodies may have been made by the mother during the current pregnancy or during an earlier pregnancy.

Transfusion from the father to an older child would not be expected to cause this problem.

In some instances it may be possible to detect antibodies in the baby to the father's red blood cells by testing before the transfusion but this will not pick up all antibodies.

Older children may already have been sensitised against the mother's blood cells as there is some passage of cells from the mother into the baby during pregnancy. This fact is less well known than the recognised risk of the baby's cells passing into the mother's bloodstream but also carries some potential risks. For example, if cells from the mother are transfused into an older child there is a possibility that this will act as a 'booster' injection. The child may develop high levels of antibodies within a few days and break down the mother's transfused blood cells.

Transfusion of partner's blood to a patient who is or has been pregnant can cause acute reactions similar to those seen in the neonatal situation as the woman may have developed potent antibodies to the partner's cells as a result of the pregnancy. In addition, the woman may develop antibodies *after* the transfusion, which may cause problems to the baby in future pregnancies.

For neonatal transfusions, paedipacks should be provided, drawn only from donors who have donated previously and divided into several aliquots to minimise the risks further.

The administration of blood can be a major worry for both patients and relatives. The decision to give a transfusion should never be taken lightly. Transfusion within the UK is extremely safe in respect of transmission of viral infections. We do not know about risk of vCJD transmission at present. It is important not to create another avoidable risk for the patient because of immune risks due to the transfusion of blood from relatives.

Appendix 5
Jehovah's Witness patients

Information for clinical staff

Each patient has a right to be treated with respect and staff must be sensitive to their individual needs, acknowledging their values, beliefs and cultural background.

- Clinical practitioners must be aware of the Jehovah's Witness' beliefs in relation to receiving blood or blood products and of the non-blood, medical alternatives to transfusion that may be applicable.
- It is essential that each Jehovah's witness patient who is competent is given the opportunity to discuss treatment options with a responsible doctor under a guarantee of strict clinical confidentiality.
- It is essential that any agreement to preserve total clinical confidentiality be strictly honoured.
- Jehovah's Witnesses are encouraged to carry a card at all times that details their wishes about medical care. Staff must take full note of this card. They must ensure also that the patient signs the appropriate form indicating his or her refusal to receive blood or blood components.
- Individual Jehovah's Witnesses may accept treatments such as dialysis, cardiopulmonary bypass, organ transplants, non-blood replacement fluids or plasma derivatives.

Elective Surgery

At time of referral (surgical outpatient department)

All patients: check FBC. If abnormal arrange appropriate investigation and correct any haematinic deficiency.

If the procedure and the patient's condition are such that the clinician would normally request that blood is crossmatched, discuss with the patient (or parents/guardian) which of the available blood-sparing options and alternatives would be acceptable, e.g., cell salvage, acute normovolaemic haemodilution, erythropoietin, fibrin sealant, albumin or other colloid solutions

Six weeks preoperatively
Adults:
- Oral iron

Children:
- 1-5 years: sodium feredate elixir* 2.5 ml tid
- 6-12 years: sodium feredate elixir 5 ml tid
  * *(sodium feredate sugar free elixir 27.5 mg Fe/5 ml)*

10 days preoperatively to 5 days postoperatively
- Erythropoietin if the anticipated blood loss >15-20% blood volume.

Use according to manufacturer's information

7 days preoperatively
- Stop NSAID and aspirin

3 days preoperatively
- Stop warfarin where possible

At operation
- Optimise anaesthetic technique - hypotension, hypothermia
- Maximise haemostasis: surgical, antifibrinolytics, fibrin sealant
- Conserve blood use: ANH, intraoperative, postoperative blood salvage.

Authors and reviewers

Editor:

D B L McClelland
Clinical Director
Edinburgh & South East Scotland Blood Transfusion Service
Royal Infirmary
Edinburgh EH3 9HB

Section Authors:

J A J Barbara
Consultant in Microbiology to
    the National Blood Service,
    England
North London Blood
Transfusion Centre
Colindale Avenue
London NW9 5BG

A Gray
Project Manager
Effective Use of Blood
Scottish National Blood
    Transfusion Service
Ellen's Glen Road
Edinburgh EH17 7QT

K R Palmer
Consultant Gastroenterologist
Western General Hospital
Crewe Road
Edinburgh EH4 2XU

W D Plant
Consultant Renal Physician
Department of Medicine
Royal Infirmary of Edinburgh
Lauriston Place
Edinburgh EH3 9YW

P Clarke
Consultant Haematologist
East of Scotland Blood
    Transfusion Service
Ninewells Hospital
Dundee DD1 9SY

M F Murphy
Chair of NBS Clinical Policies
    Group
Consultant
National Blood Service
John Radcliffe Hospital
Headington
Oxford OX3 9DU

D H Pamphilon
Consultant Haematologist
National Blood Service
Southmead Road
Bristol BS10 5ND

S Rogers
Consultant Haematologist
Victoria Hospital
Hayfield Road
Kirkcaldy KY2 5RA,
Fife

C J Sinclair
Consultant Anaesthetist
Cardiothoracic Surgery:
    Wards 17/18
Royal Infirmary of Edinburgh
Lauriston Place
Edinburgh EH3 9YW

K Soldan
Infection Survey Officer
PHLS CDSC
National Blood Service
61 Colindale Avenue
London NW9 5EQ

A A M Todd
Consultant Haematologist
Clinical Apheresis Unit
Glasgow Royal Infirmary
Castle Street
Glasgow G4 0SF

J P Wallis
Consultant Haematologist
Department of Haematology
Freeman Hospital
High Heaton
Newcastle Upon Tyne NE7 7DN

F G Williams
Chief Executive
Welsh Blood Service
Ely Valley Road
Talbot Green
Pontyclun CF72 9WB

P L Yap
Consultant Immunology
Clinical Services Directorate
Edinburgh & South East
    Scotland Blood Transfusion
    Service
Royal Infirmary
Edinburgh EH3 9HB

N A Smith
Consultant Haematologist
National Blood Service
Vincent Drive
Edgbaston
Birmingham B15 2DG

M L Turner
Consultant Haematologist
Edinburgh & South East Scotland
Blood Transfusion Service
Royal Infirmary
Edinburgh EH3 9HB

T S Walsh
Consultant Anaesthetist
Department of Anaesthetics,
Intensive Care & Pain Medicine
Royal Infirmary of Edinburgh
Lauriston Place
Edinburgh EH3 9YW

L M Williamson
Lead Consultant
National Blood Service
East Anglian Blood Transfusion
    Centre
University of Cambridge
Long Road
Cambridge CB2 2PT

Figures drawn by:

S P Lumley
Associate Specialist
North of Scotland Blood Transfusion Service
Raigmore Hospital
Inverness IV2 3UJ

Reviewers:

Martin Bruce
National Quality Manager
SNBTS Headquarters
Ellen's Glen Road
Edinburgh EH17 7QT

R H A Green
Clinical Director
West of Scotland Blood Tranfusion
    Centre
25 Shelley Road
Glasgow G12 0XB

S Reid
Clinical Services Directorate
Edinburgh & South East Scotland
Blood Transfusion Service
Royal Infirmary
Edinburgh EH3 9HB

D Stainsby
National Blood Service
Newcastle Centre
Holland Drive
Barrack Road
Newcastle upon Tyne NE2 4NQ

J P Wallis
Consultant Haematologist
Department of Haematology
Freeman Hospital
High Heaton
Newcastle upon Tyne NE7 7DN

A Gray
Project Manager
Effective Use of Blood
Scottish National Blood
    Transfusion Service
Ellen's Glen Road
Edinburgh EH17 7QT

B R Gunson
Patient's Association
PO 935
Harrow
Middlesex HA1 3YJ

E A E Robinson
Medical Director
National Blood Authority
Oak House
Reeds Crescent
Watford
Herts WD1 1QH

A A M Todd
Consultant
Clinical Apheresis Unit
Glasgow Royal Infirmary
Castle Street
Glasgow G4 0SF

L M Williamson
Lead Consultant
National Blood Service
East Anglian Blood Transfusion
    Centre
University of Cambridge
Long Road
Cambridge CB2 2PT

Blood Transfusion Centres

	Tel No.	Fax No.
National Blood Authority (HQ)	01923 486800	01923 486801
Scottish National Blood Transfusion Centre (HQ)	0131 556 5700	0131 536 5701
Newcastle Blood Transfusion Centre (Northern)	0191 219 4400	0191 219 4505
Leeds Blood Transfusion Centre (Yorkshire)	0113 214 8600	0113 214 8737
Sheffield Blood Transfusion Centre (Trent)	01142 034800	01142 034911
Cambridge Blood Transfusion Centre (East Anglia)	01223 548000	01223 548136
North London Blood Transfusion Centre (Colindale)	0208 258 2700	0208 258 2970
Essex Blood Transfusion Centre (Brentwood)	01277 306000	01277 306128
South Thames Blood Transfusion Centre (Tooting)	0208 258 8300	0208 258 8453
Southampton Blood Transfusion Centre (Wessex)	0238 029 6700	0238 029 6760
Oxford Blood Transfusion Centre	01865 447900	01865 447915
Bristol Blood Transfusion Centre (South West)	0117 991 2000	0117 991 2002
Birmingham Blood Transfusion Centre (West Midlands)	0121 253 4000	0121 253 4003
Liverpool Blood Transfusion Centre (Mersey)	0151 551 8800	0151 551 8895/96
Manchester Blood Transfusion Centre (North West)	0161 251 4200	0161 251 4319/4331
Lancaster Blood Transfusion Centre (North West)	01524 306221	01524 206222
Cardiff Blood Transfusion Centre (Wales)	01443 622000	01443 622199
Belfast Blood Transfusion Centre (Northern Ireland)	028 90321414	028 90439017
Aberdeen Blood Transfusion Centre (North East Scotland)	01224 685685	01224 662200
Dundee Blood Transfusion Centre (East Scotland)	01382 645166	01382 641188
Edinburgh Blood Transfusion Centre (North East Scotland)	0131 536 5300	0131 536 5352
Glasgow & West of Scotland Blood Transfusion Centre (Gartnavel)	0141 357 7700	0141 357 7701
North of Scotland Blood Transfusion Centre (Inverness)	01463 704212	01463 237020
Dublin Blood Transfusion Board	00 353 1 660 3333	00 353 1 660 3419
Cork Blood Transfusion Board	00 353 21 496 8799	00 353 21 431 3014

Glossary of terms and abbreviations

Apheresis (single donor) platelet concentrate
Platelets prepared by apheresis of the donor

Apheresis (single donor) plasma
Plasma prepared by apheresis of the donor

Artificial colloid solutions
Gelatins, dextrans, hydroxyethyl starch

Anti-D immunoglobulin
Human IgG preparation containing a high level of antibody
to the Rh D antigen

Autologous transfusion
General term for several techniques e.g.,
preoperative blood donation
perioperative isovolaemic haemodilution
salvage from operation site (intra-operative)
salvage from operation site (postoperative)

BCSH
British Committee for Standards in Haematology

Blood components
Whole blood, red cells, plasma, platelets, cryoprecipitate
prepared in the Regional Transfusion Centre

Blood products:
Any therapeutic product derived from human wholeblood
or plasma donations

CABG
Coronary artery bypass grafting

CJD
Creutzfeldt-Jakob Disease

CMV
Cytomegalovirus

Colloid solutions (artificial colloids)
Gelatin; Dextran, starch preparations: Appendix 2, page 113

Crystalloid solutions
Saline, Ringer's lactate etc.

DAGT
Direct antiglobulin test (Coombs' test) - sensitive method to detect red cell bound antibody

DIC
Disseminated intravascular coagulation

Epoietin
Approved name for recombinant human erythropoietin

EPO
Abbreviation for erythropoietin

FFP
Fresh frozen plasma. Plasma that is frozen within a specific time period after collection and stored in the frozen state until thawed for transfusion or crushed for fractionation

GvHD
Graft-versus-host disease

HAV
Hepatitis A virus

HBV
Hepatitis B virus

HCV

Hepatitis C virus

HGV-C or GBV-C

Hepatitis G virus; a recently described virus of uncertain significance

HTLV I

Human T-cell leukaemia virus type I

Human parvovirus B19

A non-enveloped virus transmissible by blood products and potentially pathogenic in some groups of patients

Kleihauer test

Acid elution of blood film to allow counting of fetal cells in maternal blood

Massive transfusion

Transfusion in acute haemorrhage, defined variously as replacement of 1 blood volume within 24 hours, replacement of 1 blood volume with whole blood in 24 hours, etc.

NANB hepatitis

Non A non B hepatitis: former operational term for the most common class of post-transfusion hepatitis. Now known to be largely due to hepatitis C virus, and >80% eliminated by HCV screening of donations

Plasma fractions

Partially or highly purified human plasma proteins prepared from pooled human plasma under pharmaceutical manufacturing conditions and generally licensed by MCA

PTH

Post-transfusion hepatitis

PTP

Post transfusion purpura

Recovered plasma
>Plasma prepared from individual donations of whole blood

Recovered ('random donor')
>Platelets prepared from individual donations of whole blood
>platelet concentrate

Red cells
>in the text of this book, the term is used for any red cell
>component unless otherwise stated

Rh D
>The most immunogenic antigen of the Rhesus blood group
>system

Saline
>Sodium chloride intravenous infusion 0.9%

TPH
>Transplacental haemorrhage

TTP
>Thrombotic thrombocytopenic purpura

Viral inactivation
>Additional manufacturing step in making blood products:
>validated to remove or substantially reduce infectivity
>for specified viruses. Some viruses may not be reliably
>inactivated by all the current methods

Index

Blood products are indicated in **bold** type.
Page numbers relating to mentions in tables or figures are in ***bold italics***.

thrombotic thrombocytopenic purpura
(TTP) 74, 75
tranexamic acid 46, 56
transfusion
  for acute blood loss 47–48
  adverse effects *see* adverse events
  autologous 39, 43–44, 131
  and bleeding 49
  in chronic anaemia 61–62
  clinical response 34
  compatibility 23–24
  complications 51-53 *see also* adverse
    events
  errors 26, 30, 92
  evidence-based practice 1–2
  for gastrointestinal bleeding 53–56
  guidelines 39
  immunological consequences 57
  infants and neonates 81–85
  infusion rate 35, 93, 95
  intraoperative 41
  intrauterine 66
  massive 51, 133
  minimising the need for 42–44, 82,
    103
  observation essential 34
  in obstetric haemorrhage *80*
  platelets 56
  postoperative 42
  procedures 25–27
  reactions 92–102
  recording reasons 25, 34, 41
  restrictive or liberal policies 40
  staff involved 1, 28, 79
  threshold and target haemoglobin level
    40, *41*
transfusion-associated graft-versus-host
disease (TA-GvHD) 66–67, 100, 122
transfusion-dependent anaemia 61
transfusion-related acute lung injury
  (TRALI) 53, 92, 93, *96*, 98
transfusion-transmissible infections 2,
  103-108
Trasylol *see* aprotinin
trauma resuscitation, procedures 48
treponemal infections 107
Trypanosoma cruzi 108
TT virus 105

type and screen 28, 29

urticaria *see* allergic reactions

variant Creutzfeldt-Jacob disease (vCJD)
  1-2, 3, 7, 11, *19*, 105
varicella zoster *76–77*
varices, chronic liver disease 53, *55*
vasculitis 74, 75
vCJD *see* variant Creutzfeldt-Jacob
  disease
viral infections 2–3, 103–108
virus-inactivated products 60, 103, 134
vitamin B12 61
volume expanders *see* colloids;
  crystalloids
von Willebrand factor 60
von Willebrand's disease 46, 60–61
  see also haemophilia

Waldenstrîm's macroglobulinaemia 74
warfarin 43, 126
Wegener's vasculitis 74
white cells *see* leucocytes
WHO terminology for blood products
  ix
whole blood, storage and administration
  12
whole blood, leucocyte depleted *13–14*

Yersinia enterocolitica 107
young patients 40, 41

Acknowledgement

The manuscript typed by Mrs Irene McKechnie.